Born in 1950, Rowan Williams was educated in Swansea (Wales) and Cambridge. He studied for his theology doctorate in Oxford, after which he taught theology in a seminary near Leeds. From 1977 until 1986 he was engaged in academic and parish work in Cambridge, before returning to Oxford as Lady Margaret Professor of Divinity. In 1990 he became a Fellow of the British Academy.

In 1992 Professor Williams became Bishop of Monmouth, and in 1999 he was elected as Archbishop of Wales. He became Archbishop of Canterbury in late 2002 with ten years' experience as a diocesan bishop and three as a primate in the Anglican Communion. As Archbishop, his main responsibilities were pastoral – whether leading his own diocese of Canterbury and the Church of England, or guiding the Anglican Communion worldwide. At the end of 2012, after ten years as Archbishop, he stepped down and moved to a new role as Master of Magdalene College, Cambridge.

Professor Williams is acknowledged internationally as an outstanding theological writer and teacher as well as an accomplished poet and translator. His interests include music, fiction and languages.

Rowan Williams

Luminaries: Twenty lives that illuminate the Christian way

First published in Great Britain in 2019

Society for Promoting Christian Knowledge
36 Causton Street
London SW1P 4ST
www.spck.org.uk

British Library Cataloguing-in-Publication Data
A catalogue record for this book is available from the British Library

ISBN 978–0–281–08295–7
eBook ISBN 978–0–281–08160–8

1 3 5 7 9 10 8 6 4 2

Typeset by Geethik Technologies, India
Printed in Great Britain by TJ International

Produced on paper from sustainable forests

Contents

Introduction   vii

St Paul (*c*.5–*c*.67)
A man of passions   1

St Alban (third century)
The duty of a Christian   7

St Augustine of Hippo (354–430)
Teacher of the inner life   14

St Augustine of Canterbury (*c*.530–604)
Apostle to the English   21

St Anselm of Canterbury (*c*.1033–1109)
The justice of God   29

Meister Eckhart (1260–1328)
The mystery of Godness   36

Thomas Cranmer (1489–1556)
'The word of God is not bound'   44

William Tyndale (1494–1536)
God and the economy of debt   53

St Teresa of Avila (1515–82)
A lived theology   59

John Milton (1608–74)
From heroism to fidelity   71

Contents

William Wilberforce (1759–1833)
The moral state   80

Charles Dickens (1812–70)
The truth of exaggeration   89

Florence Nightingale (1820–1910)
The light of life   95

Sergei Bulgakov (1871–1944)
Politics, art and prayer   101

Edith Stein (1891–1942)
Thinking in solidarity   107

Michael Ramsey (1904–88)
True humanism   112

Dietrich Bonhoeffer (1906–45)
Freedom, necessity and glory   119

Simone Weil (1909–43)
Waiting on God   124

Etty Hillesum (1914–43)
A compulsion to kneel   131

St Óscar Romero (1917–80)
God has injected himself into history   136

Notes   143

Introduction

This book is a series of reflections on people's stories, and sometimes also their writings. It's not a book that tells people's stories or looks at their writings as a matter of historical interest alone. It's about *deciphering* stories: deciphering stories and writings that themselves set out to decipher the world and help to illuminate it. It's an attempt to make sense of lives that make sense of the world, and which may also help us make sense of God.

That ought not to be a surprising or novel observation, because, of course, that is very much what is going on in the New Testament. It's no accident that Jesus is remembered as a storyteller in the Gospels, and not just as a teacher of general truths. We know that one of the most distinctive things about his teaching was his use of *narrative*. And it's significant in this connection that in the story of Jesus after the resurrection walking with the disciples on the road to Emmaus, what Jesus actually does is retell a story.

'Don't you know', say the disciples to Jesus, 'what's been happening? Don't you know the story of what's been happening in Jerusalem in recent days? You must be the only person who doesn't.'

In response Jesus says, in effect, 'I'm going to tell you the *whole* story.' And, 'beginning with Moses and all the prophets', he retells the story of what's been happening in Jerusalem in recent days until it makes sense; and, as bread is broken across the table, the disciples realize that a completely new kind of sense has been made of the whole of *their* story, their life and their environment, by this encounter with the risen Christ (Luke 24.13–35).

The resurrection enables people to retell the whole story of God's dealings with his people throughout the centuries as this gradually comes to its focus and climax in the death and resurrection of Jesus. In the light of Jesus' storytelling, the disciples rush back to Jerusalem to help everybody else see their stories all over again. This is one way to describe how the proclamation of the good news works, one way in to the whole Christian doctrine of redemption. To talk of ourselves as redeemed sinners is to talk of ourselves as having learned how to tell our story *differently*. Or, to put it in a rather condensed way, the unredeemed sinner is a person who has not yet learned how to tell a different story about themselves, but only the story of failure, the story of loss, the story of guilt.

The Orkney poet George Mackay Brown has a short story – 'Brig o' Dread' – that is relevant to this, a story that is effectively about purgatory. It begins by depicting a man apparently lost somewhere on fog-laden uplands. He looks out on to a desolate and unsignposted landscape. There are at first no clues about which direction to take. Meanwhile, his memory is working overtime as he stumbles through the fog – the memories of things that have gone wrong in his life.

As the story unfolds, it is subtly made clear that this man is dead, and he doesn't know where he's going because he can't yet tell a story about his life that makes sense and moves towards reconciliation and homecoming. He discovers that he must bring to the surface memories that are profoundly hurtful and humiliating, not only the comfortable self-images he has been nurturing, and he must rehearse the truth of these until the story begins to take fresh shape. The reader begins to grasp that what the man has to do is to allow something *new* into that story, some moment of hope or love or reconciliation which he can't generate for himself.

At the end of the story, some corner of the fog is beginning to lift; the lights of an inhabited house appear in the landscape, though the labour continues. There might, after all, be a place to live, there might be a story to tell, but until something new comes in to change the story, we are trapped, stuck with the story we have been telling ourselves.

George Mackay Brown was a practising Catholic who understood something of the doctrine of purgatory. Whatever may be our view of purgatory in traditional doctrinal terms, the truth is that we all inhabit purgatories of one sort or another in our own lives on earth. A central aspect of that purgatorial experience is to be stuck in stories we don't know the way out of. And what the Christian gospel says – if we have ears to hear – is that there is something that can enter the apparent deadlock, the apparent stand-off with the stories we tell ourselves about ourselves, that will take them to a different conclusion. That something is the presence of the redeeming Christ.

So you may perhaps see why I suggest that Christian faith is the practice of making sense of lives that make sense of the world. Jesus tells stories so as to change people's world. There he is, physically confronting his audience, saying, 'At the end of this story, you will not be where you were at the beginning.' Think of the parables in that light, especially the great parables recorded in Luke's Gospel: these stories are designed to take you out of your depth and invite you to think afresh of who and where you are. The parables of Jesus push us towards getting away from the clichés in which we imprison ourselves, towards taking us into another world, or several other worlds, where we don't yet know the *end* of our story and where the categories and conventions we've been taking for granted don't automatically apply.

It is with this understanding of the power and purpose of story in mind that I offer the following reflections on the lives of people whose stories have the power to break open some of the categories that invite the reader into a new world. These are people whose lives seem to me to be 'theological' lives, lives worth thinking about because they make sense in often critical, desperate or unusual situations. Sometimes their own words, their own 'telling' of themselves or their reflection on their experience, is the main thing that strikes; sometimes it's the bare record of their lives or deaths. And as we think about those stories and try to make sense of them, we may find that there are ways in which telling these stories can become a dimension of what we offer to one another and to the wider world as good news.

The people I've written about here are a very diverse group indeed, and there is no special principle of selection; a book ten times this length could easily be put together, and many readers will ask, 'Why not so-and-so?' The only answer is that these are figures I have been invited to think about and celebrate over the years, and figures who are for me, in various ways, beacons of illumination: people who lived lives that open up perspectives and horizons for the rest of us that are unpredictable and enriching. Some are people I think I should have liked to spend time with, others are frankly not! The point is not that these are straightforwardly good and attractive folk, only that they are people who let the light through, even in lives that are sometimes flawed and compromised.

Sharing stories like these in the light of the great story that Jesus shares on the road to Emmaus – and the great story that Jesus *is* – is just one way of communicating what I think is a central part of the good news. The world is more than you ever thought, *you* are more than you ever thought, God is more than you could *begin* to think, and you are not trapped in the story you tell yourself about yourself; that vision is a gift worth sharing.

St Paul

c.5–c.67

A man of passions

What kind of a person was St Paul? What do we know of his personal life? St Luke in the Acts of the Apostles calls him 'a *young* man named Saul' (Acts 7.58). If Stephen was killed in Jerusalem around the year AD 34, as seems likely, not very long after Jesus' crucifixion, then Paul was a 'young' man at this date. In the ancient world, you definitely stopped being 'young' at the age of 40; so we can conclude that in AD 34 Saul of Tarsus was, at most, in his thirties. It is a reasonable guess that he was about the same age as Jesus would have been, perhaps a little younger. Jesus, born in probably 7 or 6 BC, would have been between 33 and 40 at the time of his crucifixion. If Paul was a little younger, born after 6 BC, he was perhaps in his mid-thirties when we first meet him.

And his personal life? We know from the first letter to Corinth that he did not have a wife; that he had chosen not to have a wife to take with him on his travels, contrasting his situation with that of St Peter and others (1 Corinthians 7.8; 9.5). Given his rabbinic upbringing, the most likely theory is that he was a widower, and nothing in the first letter to Corinth tells against that – when he writes to single people, he explicitly includes both those who have never been married and widowers. I think there is a reasonable case for thinking that that was his own situation.

We know that his health was uncertain. We know that when he arrived in Galatia, so he tells us in his letter to Christians in the region (Galatians 4.13–14), he was suffering from an ailment that was something of a challenge to his hearers. What was this? It could have been epilepsy, as some have suggested; it could also have been some kind of eye disease that would have distorted his face. Interestingly, there are a couple of occasions in the Acts of the Apostles where Paul is described as 'looking intently', or 'peering' or 'screwing up his eyes' (for example, Acts 23.1); and it may be no accident that he describes the Galatians as having been ready to tear out their eyes and give them to him (Galatians 4.15). It is not at all unlikely that he suffered from one of the countless forms of eye disease carried by parasites in the Middle East, which again would explain why he looked rather unattractive, with swollen eyes and perhaps pus-laden eyelids. Famously, in his second letter to Corinth, he writes (12.7ff.) of having been given a 'thorn in the flesh' – a long-standing ailment which was humiliating and restricting for him. Whether it was epilepsy, eye disease, lameness or some other kind of disability, we don't know. We do know, though, that his health was a matter of concern and seems regularly to have got in the way of his work.

We don't know what he looked like, but there is an intriguing text from quite early in the second century, originating in Asia Minor, which preserves a description of Paul as he approached the city, about to meet the formidable Thekla, one of his early female converts according to this post-biblical tradition.[1] We are told that he was a little man, bow-legged, thin-faced, hook-nosed, bald, with heavy eyebrows meeting in the middle; and this is how he is invariably depicted in the most ancient Byzantine artistic tradition and in icons of him up to the present day. Whether there is any historical background to it, we can have no idea, but it has felt plausible to generations.

And as a personality? A passionate man, powerfully, even overwhelmingly, impressive in some ways, despite his admitted weakness as a public speaker (2 Corinthians 10.10; 11.6); and sometimes, on the basis of the letters, manipulative and possessive. When his anger ran away with him he could be seriously abusive towards his enemies (Galatians 5.12 is one of the more dramatic examples); even when his anger wasn't quite running away from him, he could be fairly fierce. Beginning a chapter in his letter to the Galatians (3.1) with the words 'You idiots' is perhaps not the best way of getting the sympathy of his readers. But that forcefulness, that passion, is also shown in the way he expressed his fury at the way in which people he loved were being manipulated or mistreated by others. And whenever you are tempted to lose patience with Paul, turn to some of those passages, especially in 2 Corinthians (such as 11.20–21), where he lists the abusive activities of some of his rivals, and says, in effect, with massive sarcasm, 'Would you like *me* to treat you like that? I'm sorry: I'm not strong enough.'

Just a little before this (11.11), he speaks of the efforts and sacrifices he has made for his flock, and ends, 'Do you think I do this because I don't love you? God knows I do!' And it is this sense of warmth, of generous indignation on behalf of others, that is finally one of the most compelling features of Paul's personality – again in 2 Corinthians (11.29), he writes, 'Is there anybody who is made to stumble in their faith, and I do not burn with indignation?' You sense the profound instinctive generosity of the man underlying all the passion and the anger and the occasional manipulative or savage moment.

It is always worth remembering that Paul didn't know he was writing the Bible; that is to say, when he was writing (or rather dictating) his letters, what we read is a flow of argument which, because Paul was an emotional man, sometimes gets so tangled in its expression that a sentence breaks off and you have to start all over again. It can be hard to follow his grammar, and there are some places where sentences are not quite complete. Again, there can be a point, as in the argument in 1 Corinthians about women covering their heads in public meetings (11.16), where Paul seems to realize that he has got himself into far too complicated a place to explain fully, so breaks off and says, 'If anyone wants to argue further about this, all I have to say is that I don't know anyone who does it' – and moves on hastily.

He didn't know he was writing the Bible, which doesn't mean that this is not inspired Scripture; it simply means that Paul was not taking care over the details of his composition. There are passages of enormous elegance and eloquence: the great hymn about love in 1 Corinthians 13, known to every reader of the New Testament; passages where you can see he is working on how he says things and making it very beautiful; but also passages where he is so absorbed in his wrestling with the nature and purposes and presence of God that the grammar and some of the logical footwork disappear over the horizon.

But that is part of the humanity of Paul. He is unmistakably, in his letters, a three-dimensional figure, one of the people in the ancient world we know most about, and certainly one of the very few, apart from emperors and great public men, that we can apprehend with this degree of personal vividness. He is not, therefore, as they say, a plaster saint. He was a man of deep emotions and, like all people of deep emotions, clearly found it quite complicated to operate in a very rigid and restrictive social world. But he was also a man who, out of all that passion and that sense of living among anguished contradictions, would bring to birth in his thinking and writing a world which was indeed, as his opponents protest in the Acts of the Apostles (17.6), a world turned upside down.

From Meeting God in Paul *(London: SPCK, 2015), pp. 17–22.*

St Alban

Third century

The duty of a Christian

Earlyish in the fifth century, a bishop from France visited Britain to help sort out some local theological problems. Among other things, he is supposed to have helped the British defeat an army of invading barbarians (Picts and Saxons) by shouting 'Alleluia' at the top of their voices. A slightly more reliable memory is that he made a point of visiting the shrine of the first Christian martyr in Britain, Alban, and we're told that he took back to France some soil from the site of the martyrdom.

It's clear that the memory of Alban was a powerful one, extremely important for the Church in Britain. Various writers mention the martyrdom and the shrine, and a fairly full narrative about Alban was current by the sixth century.

The most familiar version of this is given by the eighth-century historian, the Venerable Bede, in his great history of the Church in England. According to this record, Alban was a pagan Roman citizen living in the Roman garrison town of Verulamium, and gave shelter to a Christian priest who was trying to escape persecution.

Inspired by the priest's example, Alban decided to become a Christian. He and the priest swapped clothes, and Alban was arrested on the assumption that he was the fugitive priest.

When he was examined before the magistrate, says Bede, the magistrate asked him, 'What is your name, your race and your family?' A good Roman magistrate would need to know these things. It was not a good idea to execute one of the gentry without realizing it. Roman society was heavily based on patronage, on who you knew, and if you offended or injured someone with powerful connections, your professional future might be at stake. The magistrate really needed to know who this man was.

And Alban replied, famously, 'I am a Christian and I stand ready to do my Christian duty . . . My name is Alban and I shall always adore and worship the true and living God.'[1] The good news for the magistrate who was about to sentence him to death was that he didn't have to worry about retribution from Alban's friends and family. Nobody was going to come after him, nobody was going to ruin his life because of the execution, because Alban was a Christian and his *officia*, his duties and responsibilities, were Christian ones. That's to say that his duties were not just to his friends and family, to the system of patrons and clients, to the complicated world of honour and manipulation, that kept Roman society going.

What, then, might those Christian duties look like? What might that Christian loyalty be that is more than just loyalty to a system of patrons and clients?

The Christian's duty is to the body of Christ – not to the body of Christ as some sort of organized phenomenon that you can sign up to, much as you might sign up to a political party or a golf club, but to a mysterious and living community whose fullness has not yet appeared. Christian duty, Christian loyalty, is not just to the people who happen to be with you now, people you happen to be involved with here, but to a future community in which all, friends and strangers, have their place. Christian loyalty and solidarity is being with and being for those you have not yet met and a world you have not yet seen. It's why (though this is just one among many implications) Christians ought to be passionately and sacrificially concerned about the environment, for the very simple reason that we are called to be faithful to the future, even though we can't see it, to a future of harmony and reconciliation with the whole creation. Our failure to be loyal to this particular aspect of the future is one of the most crass and troubling forms of injustice that afflicts our world – not to mention our Church – today.

So you could also say that what Alban was doing was defining the kind of loyalty, the kind of duty, that properly belongs to *pilgrims*. What is the loyalty of pilgrims to the future? Pilgrims are loyal to where they are going, to the place where God's power and love have appeared. Pilgrims keep their eyes on that future, on that goal, and so are loyal not only to the people alongside them on the pilgrimage, but also to the people around the next corner of the road, knowing that those they meet around that corner are people God has given them to stand with, and to be for.

It's a good foundation story for the Christian faith in this country – a vision of Christian belonging that doesn't try to build the walls too quickly; a vision of Christians belonging with people who have not yet heard the good news, but on whose side we must be.

And the heaviest of those Christian duties laid upon us, as upon Alban, is the demand to be in loyalty, in solidarity, not only with the people we haven't yet met but also with the people who don't particularly want to be with us, and don't even want us to be for them. That's the heart and the energy of the Christian embrace of the world in which the Christian is placed. That's the

Christian duty that constantly presses up against and challenges all the loyalties we think are obvious. We might remember the very tough words of Jesus about the need to go beyond the loyalties that are most immediate for us: loyalties to family and friends. Unless, says Jesus, you have a loyalty that is greater than that, your limited and local loyalty will become something dangerous and corrupt, inward-looking and destructive. And Jesus himself not only speaks about but also acts out a loyalty to what is not yet, 'the joy that is set before him', says the writer of the letter to the Hebrews (12.2), the kingdom which he burns with passion to enter.

Our local loyalties are put under question when we come into solidarity with Jesus. We no longer know so obviously whose side we are meant to be on, because the gospel seems to say uncomfortably that the real answer is 'everybody's' – in the sense that we are to stand alongside, to pray for, to give to and to be for everyone. Anything less than that and we're back in the world of patronage and clients and influence that dictates the magistrate's question – and in our present age, back in a world of xenophobia and suspicion, fear of the other, fear of the stranger.

If Alban had been recognized as the patron saint of this country, perhaps it would have been a way of reminding our society of the terrible dangers of mis-understanding loyalty and solidarity, and of the immense, exhilarating and rather terrifying gift of being invited to open our lives, our hearts, our homes and our economies to strangers – as Alban opened his home to the man running from persecution and decided to stand in his place and risk his penalty. Perhaps it would have helped us overcome that deepest and most disturbing of contemporary pathologies – the strange and terrible fear of the refugee, the helpless stranger in our midst – that so distorts so much of our social and political life. But God, with his well-known sense of irony, has in fact given us a national patron in St George, who happens to have been what we now would call a Palestinian Arab. I wonder occasionally whether all those who fly the flag of St George with such enthusiasm these days quite realize that they are paying homage to somebody whose company might have been a little more unsettling than they imagine . . .

So Alban is a preacher of challenging good news for us, not just in his death but also in those words with which he answered the magistrate: 'I am a Christian and I stand ready to do my Christian duty.' I am a Christian and my loyalties are Christian loyalties. My solidarity is with the body of Christ, a body still in formation, whose limits I don't yet know.

It's helpful always to be reminded that our loyalty as believers is not first and foremost to 'the Church' as we see it, but to the body that is in formation, that multitude that no one can number who respond to the call of Jesus Christ, today and tomorrow and the day after. And our lives must be structured around that kind of prayerful hospitality which, today, tomorrow and the day after, resolves to be open to those whom God gives us to be with and to be for.

We thank God for Alban's witness and courageous death, and we thank him also for Alban's theology, that single proclamation in which is contained so much of the New Testament, so much of our hope and so much of our judgement: 'I am a Christian and I stand ready to do my Christian duty . . . I shall always adore and worship the true and living God.'

Based on a sermon preached on 24 June 2006 at the Festival of St Albans, St Albans Cathedral.

St Augustine of Hippo

354–430

Teacher of the inner life

If you ask the average educated Christian about Augustine of Hippo, the foremost thinker in the Western Church, who wrote mostly between around 390 and 420, they're most likely to associate him with two matters only. Wasn't he the one who made Christianity neurotic about sex? And didn't he invent the doctrine of predestination?

Yet Augustine scholarship today is more buoyant and creative than it's been for a long time, and quite a few contemporary 'postmodern' theologians would claim him as their patron. His arguments on subjects such as time and speech continue to be discussed by professional philosophers; his reflections on the nature of political life have drawn enthusiastic comment from several social commentators, especially in the USA. Why might his heritage be significant for us 1,600 years on? If he isn't just a bad influence, what ought to make us read him?

I shan't try to respond in detail to the charges about sex and predestination, though I think Augustine has had a ridiculously bad press on both from people who often have read only a tiny portion of his writing. I want rather to look at one or two themes in his work that ought to challenge contemporary Christians and contemporary society in necessary ways. These themes have to do with what he thought a *person* really was – a matter (I hardly need say) that brings together how we talk about God and how we talk about ourselves.

Augustine's *Confessions*, the story of his journey to adult Christian faith, is rightly considered the first literary work in Western culture to look systematically at how memory works. Augustine is fascinated by the fact that we are not transparent to ourselves: I don't know what I know; there are things I've learned that are somewhere in my mind, but I can't 'access' them. So I never know what is bearing down on me at any given moment. My choices and my acts are technically free (this mattered enormously to him), yet I can never fully grasp my motivation. To be a person at all is to be in search of myself, to be caught up in the continuous process of asking about myself, wondering about myself. It's this that makes human beings such an oddity in the universe.

So far, a modern reader might feel very enthusiastic. Yes, we say, our selfhood is compellingly interesting, and we need to spend plenty of time getting in touch with our inner questioning and understanding how we work. But Augustine will not let us get away with that. Certainly, our endless self-questioning is fascinating; but the whole point is that it can never arrive at a resolution. I am always incomplete; at the end of my self-searching lies a basic need and emptiness, and only when I make contact with *that* does change occur.

Most of the time, my innate restlessness makes me look for things to fill the gap, things that will tell me once and for all that I have arrived and that I'm safe. When I've attained that goal, acquired that thing or that person, I shall be whole. But the very idea that I could get to such a point is the fundamental error human beings make. And we can make it in the realm of the spiritual as much as in the realm of the material: Augustine's *Confessions* records how he looked for a solution first in the comprehensive theory of the universe offered by the Manichaean sect, then, more sensibly but still mistakenly, in the mystical experience of oneness that arose from Neoplatonic philosophy. But neither theory nor experience seemed to touch the real centre of his willing and acting; his *love* wasn't transformed.

How change came about for Augustine is a long story, but in his record of it he points to two things. Only when he realized that he couldn't by himself make a unity of his life, that he couldn't tell the full true story of who he was, only when he faced the deepest vulnerability in himself, could the truth get through. And the fact that triggered and made sense of this was the fact of Jesus. Christian faith claims that the eternal truth and wisdom of God spoke most completely in a single human life and death. God spoke the language of time. To receive his truth is neither to acquire a theory about the universe nor to escape from time into a reconciled eternity, but to embrace the struggle to be faithful within the limits of being a creature with a body and a biography.

So, in this context, not even God becomes an object that will satisfy my longing and my incompleteness. I must learn in this life to accept the fact that hunger and restlessness are part of what I am made for. To love God is not to acquire the biggest and best gratification of all but to have my whole experience of love transfigured. Instead of the manic struggle to fill the gap in my heart, which leads me to the exploitation and domination of others and of my whole world, I acknowledge that I am never going to feel cosily at one with myself, all desires gratified; my longing opens out on to the horizon of the infinite God. But the more clearly I understand what

God is (as Augustine says in one of his meditations on the Psalms), the more I know that I can't possess or fully express what he is.

What I can do, however, is walk with Jesus Christ in the risky territory of this world, trusting his gift, and not my effort, to keep me faithful. And instead of the urge to fill the gap in my heart, that gap becomes the way in which God's own love comes alive in me: I start wanting what God wants, I come to share his will to give himself. And so I begin to see other human beings in the light of God, to love them a bit more as he does, to long for their good as if it were mine. This, says Augustine, is how the passion for justice grows out of love for God: I stop taking it for granted that how I define what's good for me sets the agenda for everyone else, and I learn to see that there is no good for me that doesn't involve good for others.

It isn't a comfortable picture. It doesn't allow me to settle down with God in a spiritual Darby and Joan relationship; neither does it simply give me a tidy programme of doing good to others so that I feel good about myself. It tells me that I have to make friends with my limitations and to accept that my discipleship will always have about it some of the ache of absence and loss. God is active in the heart of my memory and God is what draws me to an unimaginable future, but he's not ever here as an object I possess. In Jesus he stands with me; as my creator, he is deeper within me than I can reach myself.

Yet he doesn't sit passively before me for me to look at. He requires me – in one of Augustine's most powerful images – to keep running after him as he rounds corner after corner ahead of me. And my deepening sense of my incompleteness is allowed gradually to wean me away from the fantasy that I have a set of individual needs that is absolutely given and must be promoted in rivalry with others. The sense of my own mystery opens up the mystery of others; the liberation from self-idolatry opens me up to communicating a love more like God's. And I become able to love people not as instruments for my gratification but for what they truly are – created beings made for God's own joy.

Out of this, for Augustine, flows a vision of how love works in the Church: a passionate, sometimes rather one-sided, emphasis on the sovereignty of grace, and a saving scepticism about what my will can achieve. This vision is a picture of God's own Trinitarian life. If we try beginning our theology with something like

Augustine's sense of what a human self really is, we may find it equally fertile as we seek to grow in that loving wisdom which he regarded as the centre of all theology, as of all holiness.

St Augustine of Canterbury

*c.*530–604

Apostle to the English

The end of the sixth century was a bleak time in Europe. The outbreak of bubonic plague mid-century had reduced populations across the continent by up to one-third in some regions. The administrative system of the Roman Empire had almost disappeared. What we now call France, Spain and northern Italy were ruled by kings drawn from the Germanic tribes that had taken over in the previous 200 years. Out beyond the western sea, in the remote British islands, Roman rule had long since vanished, and an assortment of settlers from what is now southern Denmark and northern Germany had begun to organize themselves into kingdoms. The combination of the terrible effects of plague and political and administrative chaos meant that the mood across Europe was sombre.

One of the few points of stability could be found in Rome. The old capital was not very significant in conventional political terms, but it still had symbolic status, focused in this era on the person of its bishop, who was increasingly referred to by the colloquial Latin and Greek word for 'father': *papa* – the pope. And at the end of the sixth century, it happened that the pope was an exceptional figure – a man from a senior aristocratic family with generations of administrative and diplomatic experience behind him, a man who had served with distinction as an envoy at the emperor's court, and also someone with a deep understanding of the all-important renewal of Christian devotion represented by the monastic movement.

Pope Gregory was profoundly affected by the sombre feeling in the air. Like many, he thought it likely that the world was soon coming to an end. Famines, plagues and wars were just the sorts of things that the Bible warned were signs of the end of time. And even though Gregory, like other more thoughtful and sensible theologians, wasn't keen to predict an exact date, it was obviously difficult not to feel that everything was inexorably running down. And if this were indeed the case, it was all the more important to make sure that all people, even the most remote and barbaric, had the chance to hear the Christian gospel before the Last Judgement arrived. So it wasn't surprising that he took an interest in the offshore islands to the west.

There is a well-known story that he first registered the situation in Britain when, earlier in his career, he encountered some young men from northern England in the slave markets in Rome. Told that they were from the people of the 'Angles', he responded by saying that they looked 'more like angels than Angles'.[1] When he became Pope some years later, he decided that this mysterious country where the Angles lived should be the focus of a missionary campaign.

The man chosen to lead the campaign was a monk called Augustine. We don't know anything about his life before this except that he was in a senior position at the monastery that Gregory had founded in Rome. But we can get quite a vivid picture of him from the account of his mission written a little more than a hundred years later by another monk, the historian Bede, who lived in the far north-east but had access to the traditions and documents of the community Augustine founded in Kent.

Augustine comes across as an almost endearingly nervous and anxious man. He did his best to persuade Gregory to let him turn back before he even reached Britain. He wasn't at all sure what his status was in relation to the longer-established bishops in France, who, if we read between the lines, were finding it difficult to believe that this awkward and shy Italian monk had been given the big responsibility of starting a national mission.

Once he was in position in England, Augustine pestered the Pope with queries about how he should bring his converts into line. When he met the Celtic bishops from western Britain, he wrecked the meeting by standing on his dignity and treating them as inferiors. He has all the marks of a man with minimal self-confidence.

Of course, you can't really blame him. He was isolated, in a country whose language he didn't speak and whose culture was completely unfamiliar to him. He had no one to share the burdens with except the other Italian monks who had travelled with him. You can sense that he felt very much like those first English missionaries who, in the nineteenth century, found themselves in places like Uganda, not only surrounded by suspicion – sometimes murderous suspicion – but also liable to be tripped up at any moment by cultural habits they knew nothing of.

But he must have got something right. Bede's history tells us that King Ethelbert of Kent gave Augustine and his monks a property in Canterbury, the regional capital. It sounds as though they settled near the only surviving church from the Roman period: St Martin's, where you can still see a few bits of Roman brick and stonework. There they lived a simple life, depending on the generosity of local people and pursuing an austere life of prayer (a lot of all-night vigils in St Martin's, says Bede). The unpretentious character of their life had a big impact in a tribal world in which status and visible wealth were all-important, and they began to attract sympathetic interest among the locals.

Before very long, King Ethelbert decided to be baptized. But Bede insists that he did not force anyone else into baptism, because Augustine had stressed that this must be a free and personal choice. It's a way of making it clear that what really made the difference was the quality of the life lived by the monks; it was important to the early historians to make it clear that even when princes and kings abandoned Christianity, local people still retained their trust and affection for the monks.

For writers of Bede's generation, this was significant: when monastic life became too soft or too heavily involved in the life of the society around, things went wrong – so it was vital for him to underline the converting effect of the simple life in the earliest days. In this connection, he also reproduced the letter from Pope Gregory to Augustine telling him how bishops should distribute their income between the support of their clergy and assistance for the poor. There is a strong emphasis on the bishop sharing a simple common life with other priests and keeping open house for all.

Augustine, as we've seen, was a naturally anxious man, and he was eager to consult Gregory on all sorts of things; it must have been a relief, in his isolated position, to know that he could turn to the Pope for help. How should he relate to bishops in France? (Consult them properly, says the Pope, and don't interfere where you're not asked, even when you think they're getting things wrong.) What is he to do about the differences between church customs in Rome and those in France? Which are the ones he should introduce in England? (Different churches just do things differently, says the Pope: use your common sense.) How do you put together the marriage laws of the Church and the rather different marriage customs of the local tribes in Britain? (Don't punish anyone for having followed their own customs, says Gregory, just make sure that in future they know what the rules of the Church are.)

And so it goes on, with Pope Gregory patiently assuring his worried subordinate that it's all right to baptize women when they're pregnant, and that there is no absolute prohibition against men coming to Holy Communion the morning after having intercourse with their wives. Sometimes in Gregory's replies you can almost hear him sighing or counting to 20: yet another letter about something that a sensible man should have been able to work out for himself.

But the letters are a priceless source of information about the sorts of things that Christians, even quite well-instructed and sophisticated ones, got in a tangle about. We read them through modern eyes as exhibiting an unhealthy preoccupation with sex, but it's more complicated than that. Sexual habits and taboos are one of the main things that mark off one tribal society from another, and now here was a new identity being offered to people that was more than tribal: it was a global Christian identity. Would this new identity sweep away everything that went before? Would every custom, every taboo, yield to the new system? And were *Christian* taboos universal and equally sacrosanct? These worries were really about the limits of diversity – almost, you could say, about the limits of multiculturalism.

Gregory famously encouraged Augustine to build churches on traditional pagan holy sites, even to use existing temples as churches, so that there wouldn't be too much discontinuity. But the problems wouldn't go away – and they have never been fully dealt with in the history of the Church's missionary activity. In the seventeenth century, the Church had to decide how to respond to the caste system in India and the veneration of ancestors in China. In the nineteenth and twentieth centuries, it had to sort out what obligations a newly converted polygamist might have to all his wives. Controversies still arise about whether local customs – dances and festivals – are harmless and neutral or whether they carry too much baggage from the non-Christian past. We, like Pope Gregory, may feel Augustine is overdoing the anxiety, but the issues of what makes belonging in the Christian Church something other than social or ethnic identity are real and live still.

From a talk broadcast on 17 October 2012 in the series Anglo-Saxon Portraits on BBC Radio 3.

St Anselm of Canterbury

*c.*1033–1109

The justice of God

What are we doing when we celebrate the Eucharist? First and foremost we are giving thanks to God for his great glory. We give thanks because we have learned from God in Jesus Christ that our peace and healing are to be found simply and definitively when we pray to the Father in the words of Jesus and so acknowledge the Father's glory as it deserves to be acknowledged. There is, you could almost say, an 'aesthetic' of salvation: we are whole, we are at one, when we offer a *fitting* response to the truth given to us, when we respond in complete harmony with what has been spoken to us. Christ eternally responds in such a way to the Father, the truth echoing the truth. For us, the task is to let that truthfulness of response to the Father's self-giving come alive in us. And the action of the Eucharist is no more and no less than this: as Christ's body, we both claim our identity and renew it in sharing it through the elements of bread and wine, so that Jesus the Word Incarnate lives in us and we in him, and God is fittingly thanked for who and what he is.

Perhaps that is as good a place as any to start in understanding St Anselm. Already a notable presence in the intellectual life of Europe in his day, an experienced monastic leader who had been abbot of the great community at Bec in Normandy, Anselm's time as Archbishop of Canterbury was a far from peaceful life of ecclesiastical routine. It is extraordinary that probably his most influential book, *Cur Deus Homo?* (*Why do we need a God who becomes human?*), was written while he was involved in bitter conflict with the king of England, a conflict that led him into exile and dangers of all sorts.

The work is a meditation on the necessity of the atoning work of Christ on the cross as an offering made to repair the insulted honour of God. This is terminology that may make us recoil in alarm. Doesn't this suggest a God who is obsessed with what is due to him, in a way that we should rightly condemn in a human being? What on earth does it mean to say that God cannot simply write off the offence to his honour that sin implies? Isn't all this a scheme that not only privileges justice over mercy but also treats justice itself as a narrow matter of satisfying inflexible and impersonal requirements?

Anselm himself would have found such objections strange. He knew about offended honour from his fierce dispute with King William II, in which he refused to spend money on keeping the king happy; he declared that any resources he had were set aside for the poor, and that he would not demand from the poor what they could not and should not give. Whatever was in his mind, it was *not* a picture of a God who was simply a larger version of William Rufus, a monarch demanding to be pacified at any cost. No; for Anselm, understanding the work of God presupposes that we are already attuned to the Spirit of God.

Every question needs to be treated within the landscape of God's self-definition, the truth God has told us about who we are in relationship with him, and who God is in relationship with us. This and this alone makes sense of the way in which Anselm tries to argue for the necessity of Christ's life and death on what seem to modern readers to be abstract and rather alien first principles – what God *must* have done if God is truly God and we are as we recognize ourselves to be: helpless and untruthful. In Anselm's own writing, this is simply a way of saying that once we have understood something of the nature of God – God's eternal, necessary, utterly coherent being – and once we have realized that this God is also free and loving in relation to what he has made, we begin to see that the only story that could ever be told about our salvation is one in which absolute divine freedom restored a relationship that we could not restore.

If you begin by standing in contemplative wonder before the pure and unconditioned self-consistency of God's being, and also in contemplative gratitude before the fact of grace at work – and there is no other rational place for the Christian to stand – you will, like the disciples on the Emmaus Road, begin to see that it was necessary for the Christ to suffer and so enter into his glory. No abstract first principles, then, but a perfectly specific stance before an active and wholly consistent God. Just as in his famous (so-called) argument for God's existence, Anselm is not playing with words and concepts but is exploring what is implied in the act of prayerful adoration.

So if we want to reconstruct what he argued about the redemption wrought in Christ, we need to start with this perspective. What Anselm sees is a humanity trapped in untruthfulness. We cannot give to God what it is our calling, our destiny and our gift to give: loving obedience that mirrors God's own life in our mortal context. We cannot 'honour' God in the simple sense that we cannot allow God to be God in our lives, and so we cannot allow ourselves to be ourselves.

When all is said and done about the feudal background of Anselm's thinking, we should remember how Anselm himself set his theology to work: this is the man who refused to send King William Rufus the subsidy he had demanded for a military expedition because he believed the request was an injustice – a *dishonour* – to his own tenants and bonded labourers, from whom the money had to be raised. Dishonour and injustice are about the effort to reduce another to the scope of your own needs and demands. Honour and justice are about respecting the truth of another's reality.

Thus it is that sin can be seen as a deadly deficit of *truthfulness*: there is no health in us because we cannot do what we are created to do – and it doesn't make a difference if all that God does is to say, 'Never mind.' The problem is not that God is clinging to his offended dignity but that *we* are being prevented – through our own grievous fault – from reflecting back to him his glory as we ought. We cannot live in a way that has true and objective *worth*. And that is why our salvation depends on an action that is not just apt or fitting or morally correct, but *precious* – an act of immeasurable worth. Christ's self-giving to the Father through his death on the cross is a perfect divine response to the self-giving of the Father – an infinitely precious and

beautiful response to an infinitely precious and beautiful gift, a perfect echo of the eternal outpouring of God
the Father in his generating of the Word.

But it is also a human act: Jesus' human freedom has
chosen to act out the eternal love without reserve,
accepting death as the cost of this acting out. Humanity
has at last done what it has been created to do, and so
a relation of truthfulness is at last restored. Our nature
has been made capable of echoing God's. We can give
back to God the gift he has given us: life, freedom and
love. Honour is satisfied – not in the sense that some
impersonal and inflexible requirement has been met,
some divine box ticked, but because justice has been
done to God himself by creation and so justice has been
done to creation, and especially to the human creation.

Here is Anselm theologizing as he loves to do, on his
knees and in the context of the Spirit-filled sacramental
life of the body of Christ:

> Taste the goodness of your Redeemer, be on fire with
> love for your Saviour. Chew the honeycomb of his
> words, suck their flavour which is sweeter than sap . . .
> Chew this, bite it, suck it, let your heart swallow it, when
> your mouth receives the body and blood of your
> Redeemer. Make it in this life your daily bread, your
> food, your way-bread . . . As the sun you gave me light,

and showed me what state I was in. You threw away the leaden weight which was dragging me down . . . And I who was bent down you made upright in your sight, saying, 'Be of good cheer. I have redeemed you. I have given my life for you.' . . . Because you have made me, I owe you the whole of my love; because you have redeemed me, I owe you the whole of myself; because you have promised so much, I owe you all my being . . . I pray you, Lord, make me taste by love what I taste by knowledge; let me know by love what I know by understanding. I owe you more than my whole self, but I have no more, and by myself I cannot render the whole of it to you. Draw me to you, Lord, in the fullness of love. I am wholly yours by creation; make me all yours, too, in love.[1]

A sermon preached on 23 April 2009 at a Eucharist held at Canterbury Cathedral, attended by the abbot and prioress of the Abbey of Notre Dame du Bec, to celebrate the 900th anniversary of the death of St Anselm of Canterbury.

Meister Eckhart

1260–1328

The mystery of Godness

Who was Meister Eckhart? We don't know a great deal about his career. He appears to have come from somewhere in mid Germany, where he returned later in life. We know that he studied at the University of Paris for a while, and that he taught there. We know also that for quite a period he was the head of the Dominican Order in Saxony. Here and there in his writings we pick up some hints of his reputation: he knows that he's sounding controversial and makes a bit of a joke of it. He died in 1327 with trouble gathering around his head as the more fussy orthodox of the day tried to have him condemned for heresy, poring over his published sermons and treatises with high hopes of a spectacular condemnation.

His subsequent reputation in the history of the Church has always been a bit ambiguous. He's difficult, he's controversial and he often gives the impression of not taking your worries quite seriously. And yet, indirectly, he had a huge influence on both sides of the Reformation, though it sounds rather curious to put it that way. Luther had read, if not Eckhart, many of Eckhart's pupils, and we can see that in some of Luther's own writing about the spiritual life. Equally, by complicated and roundabout routes, he had an influence on the Spanish mystics of the sixteenth century, right at the other end of the spectrum.

Since the sixteenth century, he hasn't been read a great deal and hasn't always been read very intelligently. He was edited extremely badly in the late nineteenth and early twentieth centuries. He appealed to some people who thought he was a kind of Buddhist in a Dominican habit and was the subject of some slightly muddled research that suggested he was really someone who believed simply in the absorption of the created spirit in God.

Better editions of his work followed in the mid-twentieth century along with some very serious research – including an epoch-making book by the great Russian Orthodox theologian Vladimir Lossky   with the result that, slowly but surely, Eckhart's reputation has begun to emerge again from the shadows. Attention has been paid not only to the German sermons, where he tends to be at his least guarded, but also to the Latin works – his professional philosophical treatises – as well as some of the Latin sermons, so as to produce a more balanced picture of someone who certainly *thought* he was an orthodox Catholic.

However, if you were to pick him up at random and read a paragraph, you might well be forgiven for thinking that 'orthodox Catholic' is not the first phrase that would spring to mind. He has one sermon entitled 'How creatures are God', which doesn't sound very promising to a nervous Christian temperament, and his style is an unusual mixture – both very colloquial and relaxed and extremely intricate and technical. We can just about see why he was a popular preacher, and he's one of the few great medieval theologians to have written and preached regularly in the language of the common people.

This is actually not a minor point about him. We don't know, for example, whether Thomas Aquinas ever uttered a word in public in any language other than Latin. We do know of Eckhart that he preached regularly in the local language to the parishes of central Germany. We know too that he was the spiritual director of a number of small lay communities, and that he was quite influential in the formation of lay common life for women in his period. The beginnings of the Beguine movement in the Low Countries owe something to the inspiration of people like Eckhart, who were prepared to act as mentors and guides for these communities of lay people living together under a loose shared rule of prayer. So, in spite of the technicality, Eckhart is not a 'remote and ineffectual don'; but this still doesn't mean that he is ever easy reading. So let me plunge in and try to explain one of Eckhart's central ideas about how we conceive of God. More than once, Eckhart suggests that we have to draw a distinction between God and what he calls *Gottheit* – a German word meaning 'Godhead' or 'Godness'. 'God', for Eckhart, is the name we give to the action that reaches to us from the divine mystery. But *Gottheit*, 'Godness', is really something about which we can say absolutely nothing and know absolutely nothing. Godness, *Gottheit*, is the utter mysteriousness of what it's like to be God. It's variously described by Eckhart in terms of an ocean, of cavernous depths and, most attractive of all perhaps, of a pot of water boiling over. The divine life is a boiling pot and it spills over into creation. Eckhart likes to use the Latin word *ebullitio* – God boiling over. The being that surges up from these mysterious depths overflows into creation and we are always and already included in the life and the being of God in some mysterious way.

So *Gottheit*, Godness, is that strange, mysterious level at which everything is already in the mind of God – but not only in the *mind* of God: it's somehow in – and here we have to search for words – the heart; the being; the surging, active, unfathomable depth of God. The possibility of everything is there in this deep, mysterious interior.

And then comes the specific divine action that emerges from this tumultuous interior divine life. 'Godness' is something about which we can say nothing whatsoever, but about *God* we can say, first of all, Father, Son and Holy Spirit, and then we can also say Creator and Redeemer. Here's an example of what Eckhart says about this:

> I take a bowl of water and put a mirror in it and set it under the disc of the sun. The sun sends forth its light-rays both from the disc and from the sun's depth, and yet suffers no diminution. The reflection of the mirror in the sun is a sun, and yet is what it is. So it is with God. God is in the soul with His nature, with His being and with His Godhead, and yet He is not in the soul. The reflection of the soul in God is God, and yet she is what she is. God *becomes* when all creatures say 'God' – then God comes to be.
>
> When I subsisted in the ground, in the bottom, in the river and fount of Godhead, no-one asked me where I was going or what I was doing: there was no-one to ask me. When I flowed forth, all creatures said 'God.'[1]

So we all begin swimming around indeterminately in the mind of God, in this mysterious depth of 'Godness', and then God acts. And God distinguishes God from creation, and there I am, and *I* can say 'God' because now I'm separate from God, I'm distinguished from God. Eckhart offers us the beautiful and rather Buddhist image of the mirror: the sun is in the mirror, but the mirror is not the sun. Does he mean by this that somehow or other God starts off as a great, undetermined soup of existence and then 'turns into' the Trinity and the creator? I don't think so, though it does sound like it sometimes. I think what he means is that we're not talking about stages in a kind of sequence; we're talking about *levels of understanding*.

His Latin texts help us a bit here, because in the Latin he distinguishes between two ways of thinking about God. God is, he says, *innominabilis*, 'unnameable', and also God is *omninominabilis*, 'all-nameable'. God has no name and God has every name. God is so mysterious that no word can apply to him; God is so full of the richness and the variety of being that any word can apply to him. At one level of understanding there's nothing we can say, there's just that infinite life which is both infinite darkness and infinite light about which we are totally at a loss to speak. And yet that life exists concretely and really as the Father, the Son and the Holy Spirit, as a life that creates and redeems. And because God establishes and engages with a created world whose life is completely shaped by what God is, all names and all realities flow to God and point to God.

That, as I said, is probably the most difficult of Eckhart's teachings, but also his most important: the difference between Godness and God – between that mysterious inner life about which we can't find any words that are any use, and *God*, which is the action by which creatures come to be distinguished from God and by which God appears to us, revealing himself as Father, Son and Holy Spirit.

It's a crucial distinction to bear in mind as we seek to serve and pray to God today. We can talk about what God does; we can't talk about what God is. Not that there is something secondary or superficial about God's life as Trinity or as creator – a sort of outward appearance of something behind which is a hinterland of complete obscurity (though, as I've said, Eckhart can give that impression at times). It's more that *what God knows the divine life to be* is something which we absolutely never have available as some sort of object for our thought. We meet God as God 'activates' all this ocean of divine life in the life of Trinity and creator and redeemer: that is what we can form some kind of picture of. But if we come to live in the eternal reality of the divine Word that flows out from the Father, we are simply carried on the wave of God's inner contemplation of and delight in what God is. How could we possibly stand to one side and turn this into an object?

From 'The Spiritual Writings of Meister Eckhart', a lecture given on 27 June 2000 to the Church Union, All Saints Church, Clifton, Bristol.

Thomas Cranmer

1489–1556

'The word of God is not bound'

It was once fashionable to decry Cranmer's liturgical rhetoric as overblown and repetitive. People often held up as typical the echoing sequences of which he and his colleagues were so fond. 'A full, perfect and sufficient sacrifice, oblation and satisfaction'; 'Have mercy upon us, miserable offenders; Spare thou them which confess their faults; Restore thou them that are penitent'; 'succour, help and comfort, all that are in danger, necessity and tribulation'; 'direct, sanctify and govern'; and, of course, 'earth to earth, ashes to ashes, dust to dust'.[1]

The liturgical puritan may well ask why it is not possible to say something once and for all, instead of circling back over what has been said, retreading the ground. And, in the same vein, many will remember the arguments of those who complained of the Communion Order in the Book of Common Prayer, that it never allowed you to move forward from penitence to confidence and thanksgiving: you were constantly being recalled to your sinful state, even after you had been repeatedly assured of God's abundant mercies.

Whether we have quite outgrown this reaction, I'm not sure. But we have at least begun to see that liturgy is not a matter of writing in straight lines. As the late Helen Gardner long ago remarked, liturgy is epic as well as drama; its movement is not inexorably towards a single, all-determining climax, but also – precisely – a circling back, a recognition of things not yet said or finished with, a story with all kinds of hidden rhythms pulling in diverse directions. And a liturgical language like Cranmer's hovers over meanings like a bird that never quite nests for good and all – or, to sharpen the image, like a bird of prey that never stoops for a kill.

The word of God is not bound. God speaks, and the world is made; God speaks, and the world is remade by the Word Incarnate. And our human speaking struggles to keep up. We need not human words that will decisively capture what the Word of God has done and is doing, but words that will show us how much time we have to take in fathoming this reality, helping us turn and move and see, from what may be infinitesimally different perspectives, the patterns of light and shadow in a world where the Word's light has been made manifest.

It is no accident that the Gospel that most unequivocally identifies Jesus as the Word made flesh is the Gospel most characterized by this same circling, hovering, recapitulatory style, as if nothing in human language could ever be a 'last' word. 'The world itself could not contain the books that should be written,' says the Fourth Evangelist, resigning himself to finishing a Gospel that is, in fact, never finishable in human terms.

Poets often reinvent their language, the 'register' of their voice. Shakespeare's last plays show him at the edge of his imagination, speaking, through Prospero, of the dissolution of all his words, the death of his magic. Yeats painfully recreates his poetic voice, to present it 'naked', as he said. Eliot, in a famous passage of the *Four Quartets*, follows a sophisticated, intensely disciplined lyrical passage with the brutal 'That was a way of putting it'. In their different ways, all remind us that language is inescapably something reflecting on itself, 'talking through' its own achievements and failures, giving itself new agendas with every word. And most of all when we try to talk of God, we are called upon to talk with awareness and with repentance. 'That was a way of putting it'; we have not yet said what there is to say, and we never shall, yet we have to go on, lest we delude ourselves into thinking we have made an end.

So the bird is bound to hover and not settle or strike. Cranmer lived in the middle of controversies where striking for a kill was the aim of most debaters. Now, of course, we must beware of misunderstanding or modernizing. He was not by any stretch of the imagination a man who had no care for the truth, a man who thought that any and every expression of Christian doctrine was equally valid; he could be fierce and lucidly uncompromising when up against an opponent like Bishop Stephen Gardiner of Winchester.

Yet even as a controversialist he shows signs of this penitent scrupulosity in language: yes, this is the truth, this is what obedience to the Word demands – but, when we have clarified what we must on no account say, we still have to come with patience and painstaking slowness to crafting what we do say. Our task is not to lay down some overwhelmingly simple formula but to suggest and guide, to build up the structure that will lead us from this angle and towards the one luminous reality. 'Full, perfect and sufficient'[2] – each word to the superficial ear capable of being replaced by either of the others, yet each with its own resonance, its own direction into the mystery, and, as we gradually realize, not one of them in fact dispensable.

We can see a poignant concomitant of this in Cranmer's non-liturgical prose. When he wrote to King Henry in unhopeful defence of Anne Boleyn and Thomas Cromwell, the convoluted sentences and sentiments show not only a constitutionally timid man struggling to be brave (and all the braver for that), but a man uncomfortably capable of believing himself deceived and of seeing the world in double perspective. What both letters in effect say is: I thought I saw the truth about this person; if I was wrong, I was more deceived than I could have thought possible. How in this world can even the King of England know the truth of his servants' hearts? I see both what I always saw and the possibility that it has all been a lie. Is this a world where we can have certainty enough to kill each other?

And in his last days, this was Cranmer's curse. If there was no easy certainty enough to kill for, was there certainty enough to die for? That habit of mind which had always circled and hovered, tested words and set them to work against each other in fruitful tension and sought to embody in words the reality of penitence and self-scrutiny, condemned him, especially in the midst of isolation, confusion, threats and seductions of spirit, to a long agony, the end of which came only minutes before his last hurrying, stumbling walk through the rain to the stake.

It is extraordinary to think of him drafting two contradictory versions of his final public confession, still not knowing what words should sum up his struggles. But at the last, it is as if he emerged from the cloud of words heaped up in balance and argument and counterpoint, knowing almost nothing except that he could not bring himself to lie in the face of death and judgement.

What he has to say is that he has 'written many things untrue' and that he cannot face God without admitting this.[3] He cannot find a formula that will conceal his heart from God, and he knows that his heart is, as it has long been, given to the God whom the Reformation let him see, the God of free grace, never bound by the works or words of men and women. Just because he faces a God who can never be captured in one set of words, a God who is transcendently holy in a way that exacts from human language the most scrupulous scepticism and the most painstaking elaboration possible, he cannot pretend that words alone will save him. 'If we deny him, he also will deny us.' He must repent and show his repentance with life as well as lips, 'forasmuch as my hand offended, writing contrary to my heart, my hand shall first be punished therefore'.[4]

He is not the only theologian to have found at the last that words failed. Aquinas, after his stroke, spoke of how all he had written seemed so much straw. Disarmingly and mischievously, Karl Barth summed up his *Church Dogmatics* to an interviewer in the words, 'Jesus loves me, this I know, for the Bible tells me so.' But neither Barth nor Aquinas would have said that there was any other way to this simplicity and near-speechlessness except by discovering in the very experience of struggling to talk about God that limit beyond which no human tongue can go. 'The word of God is not bound' (2 Timothy 2.9). At the boundaries of speech, we are only at the beginning of the fullness of the gospel.

So Cranmer draws the terrible and proper conclusion from a lifetime of skill and balance, of 'rightly dividing the word of truth' (2 Timothy 2.15, KJV): what appears bit by bit in our words about God as they are prompted and fired by the Word Incarnate is the realization of the God who is always in excess of what can be said. The rhetorical excess of repetition and rhythm is not just a stately game to decorate or dignify a basically simple act of acknowledgement directed towards God. It is the discipline that brings us to the edge of our resource; just as the insistent reversion to penitence in the Communion Order is not neurotic uncertainty but the sober expression of the truth that we never 'move on' from being saved sinners, and our amazement at God's free forgiveness has to be spoken out again and again. The edge of our resource: that is where faith belongs, and that is where the language of worship has to lead us.

It led Cranmer, as it led so many others in that nightmare age, and as it led the martyrs of our own age – Dietrich Bonhoeffer, Maria Skobtsova, Janani Luwum – to something more than a contemplative silence: to a real death. When we say that the word of God is not bound, we say that death itself can be the living speech of God, as the Word was uttered once and for all in the silence at the end of Good Friday. Cranmer speaks, not only in the controlled passion of those tight balances and repetitions in his Prayer Book, but in that chilling final quarter of an hour. He ran through the downpour to the town ditch and held out his right hand, his writing hand, for a final composition, a final liturgy. And, because the word of God is not bound, it is as if that hand in the flames becomes an icon of the right hand of Majesty stretched out to us for defence and mercy.

A sermon preached on Tuesday 21 March 2006 at the University Church of St Mary the Virgin, Oxford, to mark the 450th anniversary of the martyrdom of Thomas Cranmer, creator of the Book of Common Prayer.

William Tyndale

1494–1536

God and the economy of debt

William Tyndale, the great biblical translator and Reformed theologian, was a better theologian than he is sometimes given credit for being. People know him best as a translator, as somebody who brought back into the speech of faith in English some of that salty, vernacular touch that we find in the very best earlier, medieval writing. 'So the Lord was with Joseph, and Joseph was a lucky fellow' was one of Tyndale's great phrases from his translation of Genesis. Very often, if we look at what the Authorized Version, the King James Version, does with Tyndale, we see a very consistent rearguard action to make Tyndale's English a little bit more restrained.

But Tyndale was not just a gifted, pithy and entertaining translator; he also had a profound and far-reaching vision of the social order. For Tyndale, God was shown in the world by particular kinds of social relation. The Church is the community of those who live in Godlike relation to one another.

The Church is the community of those so overwhelmed by their indebtedness to God's free grace that they live in a state of glad and grateful indebtedness to one another. The imagery of debt and indebtedness was one that greatly interested Tyndale, and he writes about it very eloquently in his treatise on the Parable of the Unjust Steward in Luke 16, one of the most difficult parables in the New Testament. Tyndale has a very short way with it, though. For him, it is a springboard for talking about indebtedness, and he sets up this model of Christian or religious practice and thinking that struggles to keep God in our debt. That is for him the antichrist!

Any system of religious activity and thinking that tries to give us some leverage over God – 'I've never denied God a moment of my time, I hope he remembers that' – such an attitude is poisonous to true faith. What is more, it leads to what Tyndale regards as a kind of religious specialism. We develop and explore the whole range of specialist activities, which not everybody can perform, and they become the way in which we can keep God in our debt. We create religious institutions that are designed to preserve that divine indebtedness to us, and while we are doing that, we largely ignore the concrete forms of indebtedness towards other human beings to which we ought to be attending.

Tyndale puts this, of course, in blunt and practical terms. Why waste money endowing chantry chapels when you could be giving it to the poor? Why spend your life in monastic communities when your first call is to create community within the natural societies you are part of? Are not these chantries and these religious orders just an example of religious specialism trying to keep God in your debt?

I hasten to add that I don't think Tyndale was entirely right, either about chantries or about religious orders. What I am trying to tease out is why he was so angry about them. And the answer, I think, is that Tyndale was protesting against 'religion', against the separation of that sphere from other spheres of human activity. Here is Tyndale, in his 'A Pathway into the Holy Scripture':

> By faith we receive of God, and by love we shed out again. And that must we do freely, after the example of Christ, without any other respect, save our neighbour's wealth [*sic* 'welfare'] only; and neither look for reward in the earth, nor yet in heaven, for the deserving and merits of our deeds, as friars preach; though we know that good deeds are rewarded, both in this life and the life to come. But of pure love must we bestow ourselves, all that we have, and all that we are able to do, even on our enemies.[1]

Tyndale here picks up a favourite idea of Martin Luther, whose works he was reading at the time. Jesus Christ is not good and generous so that God will be nice to him. Jesus Christ is good and generous because the life of Good lives in him. So then, if we live in Christ, we aren't good and generous so as to persuade God to be nice to us. We are good and generous because that's where our life lies and we can't in one sense be anything else. So to indebtedness – and from another of Tyndale's *Doctrinal Treatises*, 'The Parable of the Wicked Mammon':

> The order of love or charity, which some dream, the gospel of Christ knoweth not of, that a man should begin at himself, and serve himself first, and then descend, I wot not by what steps. Love seeketh not her profit, 2 Cor. xii.; but maketh a man to forget himself, and to turn his profit to another man, as Christ sought not himself, nor his own profit, but ours. This term, myself, is not in the gospel; neither yet father, mother, sister, brother, kinsman, that one should be preferred in love above another. But Christ is all in all things. Every Christian man to another is Christ himself; and thy neighbour's need hath as good right in thy goods, as hasth Christ himself, which is heir and lord over all. And look, what thou owest to Christ, that thou owest to thy neighbour's need. To thy

neighbour owest thou thine heart, thyself, and all that thou hast and canst do. The love that springeth out of Christ excludeth no man, neither putteth difference between one and another.[2]

Tyndale goes on to say that our indebtedness is first to the people who are most immediately and obviously under our nose. But when he has dealt with that, he goes on: 'if thy neighbours which thou knowest be served, and thou yet have superfluity, and hearest necessity to be among your brethren a thousand miles off, to them art thou a debtor'.[3] And then, very controversially: 'yea, to the very infidels we be debtors if they need . . .'[4]

Tyndale's early Protestant editors put that in square brackets. They thought it was just a little bit too much for anybody to take on board. But Tyndale, as you can see from the enormous energy of his style, is really getting quite carried away here. If we are really indebted to other human beings, well, we are indebted to other human beings, and there's an end of it, and if they happen to be Turks or even papists, well, never mind! We owe them what we owe Christ, and we owe Christ everything, and Christ owes God his Father everything because God bestows everything upon him as he does upon us.

And so, back to where we started, the obvious corollary of this is that our generosity and our goodness come from the life of Christ living in us, and are expressed in that sense of perpetual, grateful indebtedness to all. Where there is need, there is love owing.

From Christian Imagination in Poetry and Polity *(Oxford: SLG Press, 2004), pp. 8–11. Reproduced by permission.*

St Teresa of Avila

1515–82

A lived theology

Part of the contemporary interest in the life and work
of Teresa of Avila arises from the way in which she
constantly found herself pushing against the assumptions of an exceptionally closed society. Her standing as
someone who could advise and instruct in the things
of God was, in her own day, as unusual and controversial as it could have been. We are sometimes told these
days that women are more naturally open to contemplation than men, more 'receptive'. Sixteenth-century
churchmen would have found that dangerous and offen-
sive: to them, women were naturally less intellectual
than men, and therefore needed to have their minds
carefully occupied in times of prayer, since, if they were
to be 'open' to God, if they were to abandon structured
vocal prayers, all sorts of chaotic and unsavoury impres-
sions would surge in, as they were less fully controlled
than were men.

Teresa had an even more severe problem, however.
She came from a Jewish family, at a time when people
of Jewish blood were subject to systematic hostility

and discrimination in Spain. After the Christian reconquest of the country from the Muslim princes, at the end of the fifteenth century, Christian Spaniards sought more and more fiercely for assurances of purity, in race as well as in faith; those who had converted to Christianity under duress were regarded with deep suspicion and were constantly being investigated by the authorities (the Spanish Inquisition was, in fact, created primarily to deal with this supposed problem of converted Jews secretly reverting to their ancestral religion).

Teresa's grandfather had been in trouble with the Inquisition, and she was to have her share of its attentions as well. She never spoke directly about her Jewish blood, but once we are aware of this fact about her, a good many things in her writing fall into place. One of her most passionate, even obsessive, concerns is the danger of preoccupation with 'honour', with family status and dignity. 'When this concern about lineage is noticed in a Sister, apply a remedy at once and let her fear lest she be Judas among the apostles,' she writes.[1] The reference to the apostles is very deliberate. For Teresa, the Twelve represent the ideal Christian community, without distinctions of class or kin, bound by friendship with each other and with Christ.

Friendship is, for her, a basic quality of Christian life. At 21 years of age, in 1536, Teresa entered a community in which class distinction was enshrined, a large and amorphous group where powerful personalities formed cliques and were courted for favours by the less influential and well born. For many years, she was accustomed to this atmosphere, but increasingly her unease with its implications and her growing awareness of the demands of 'friendship' with Christ pushed her in the direction of a new style of community life, one in which equality was fundamental. All could and should be on terms of friendship; all shared in the manual work of the house; all were valued independently of their background or status.

What's more, the house itself would have to be small enough not to be a great charge on a community's energy. Poverty was a serious practical matter, and Teresa was very reluctant to take on unsuitable properties or to accept benefactions that relieved the sisters from earning their living. And behind this lay a deeply theological vision: Christ invites us into his freedom and intimacy with the Father, making us his 'kin', his family. On such a basis, there can be no excuse for defending any kind of human status or family pride or racial exclusion. In one of the delightful Christmas carols she wrote for her sisters, we find this stated with great clarity:

> Comes today to ransom us
> A shepherd boy who's kin to us,
> Who's God almighty and all-glorious.
> Who out of prison snatches us,
> From Satan's clutches rescues us,
> Tom, Dick and Harry's cousin here with us,
> Who's God almighty and all-glorious.[2]

Whenever we feel intimidated by Teresa's reputation as a 'mystic', it's worth remembering this foundational theme in her work. She has no intention of setting up some complex spiritual hierarchy, in which certain elect souls are admitted to experiences that give them superior standing in the community or the Church. The essential thing is the habit of friendship with the Christ who has come among us, sharing what we are, to find friends and fellow workers. Teresa is really strikingly faithful to the gospel picture of a Christ who deliberately seeks intimacy with the friendless and invites the powerless to share in the work of the kingdom. And while, in sixteenth-century Spain, as she freely admits, there seems to be little that a community of poor women can do, she insists that their witness to the possibilities of a community in which all are equally valued is a true apostolic work. You don't have to rush off to the newly discovered missionary territories of America to have an apostolate, she says.

But what about the 'mysticism'? Teresa would not have initiated her reforms without the profound sense that God had taken an initiative in her life, and the record of her experience of God's action is largely designed to deflect the criticism of authorities who might be inclined to say that she was arrogating power to herself. Against such a charge, she can only say, I didn't *choose* to be drawn into contemplation and mission. So in her early autobiographical writings, composed for her confessors and for the Inquisition, she stresses again and again that you should never *strain* to rise beyond your present level of prayer: be faithful in what you are doing, and it may be that God will take you on.

Hence her famous analogy of the four methods of irrigating a garden: you can carry the water by hand, you can construct a water wheel, you can divert a stream to flow through or you can wait for it to rain.[3] The first three methods represent more and more sophisticated ways of conserving and concentrating energy, so that conscious effort becomes less important, but they still cannot make it rain. Rain is the most effective way of watering the garden, and in the long run it does not depend on effort. So it is with prayer: we can concentrate our work so that we become more and more 'focused' and receptive, but only God's action can ultimately bring the self harmoniously together and finally quieten its turmoils and anchor its love.

When she wrote *The Book of My Life*, she was fascinated by the extraordinary nature of God's intervention in her life – by her visions and voices, her trances and (apparently) levitations. She was inclined to identify *union* with God as a supreme experience of ecstasy. But she was writing this at a time when she was deeply involved with the early days of her reforms. As an already middle-aged woman (in her early forties), she was going through an almost unimaginable upheaval, receiving constant and powerful revelations from God as to what she could and should do to return her Carmelite order to its primitive dedication and single-mindedness, battling with suspicious and unsympathetic authorities, often finding it difficult to discover priests and bishops who would take her seriously (the Jesuits, incidentally, who had only just opened a house in Avila, provided friendship and support).

As yet, Teresa had had little opportunity of refining and developing her thoughts in conversation with a really sympathetic companion on her own level of maturity and spiritual depth. Such a companion appeared in 1567, five years after Teresa had founded her first 'reformed' Carmelite convent. He was a young Carmelite friar: John of St Matthias. When he joined Teresa's new movement in the order, he changed his dedication to John of the Cross. For several years, he was Teresa's confessor and closest adviser. She was not in awe of many people, but she *was* in awe of John (and not always, it has to be said, completely comfortable with him; there is even one document where she dares to tease him a bit for his intensity and for the uncompromising bleakness of his vision).

What John taught her can be seen in the work of her greatest maturity, written in 1576: *Interior Castle.* Here she charts, with supreme skill and confidence, the growth of the praying and loving self through seven stages (as opposed to the four of her autobiography) – seven groups of 'lodgings', *moradas* in Spanish, often unhelpfully translated 'mansions'. The soul is seen as a vast and complex dwelling, a castle built of transparent crystal, in which room leads to room in a labyrinthine progression towards the centre, where lives the King. We have to journey to that centre, and for such a journey we need a map of ourselves – which is what Teresa sets out to offer.

At every stage, she insists that the only way is forward: to stand still is to slip back. Thus there is no point where we can stop and say, 'I think I've got it sorted now'; that would be an infallible sign that we had barely started and were in fact undermining any progress made.

The pattern is the same as that of *The Book of My Life* – the gradual shift from human action and effort to divine gift. Because we are habitually not in tune with God, the impact of God upon us will be disturbing; it's almost as if we have an allergic reaction to God. Bizarre things happen to us, physically as well as psychologically, because we are so unaccustomed to God's presence. But what Teresa can now do is recognize these phenomena as *transitional*. The technicolour splendours of 'mystical experience' are not an end in themselves. She has taken fully on board John of the Cross's caution about being over-concerned with the surface manifestations of the work of God's grace, and is now quite clear that union with God is something that takes place in the depths of the soul, at a level that is normally hidden from our ordinary perception. It is manifested not in extraordinary and preternatural experiences, but in the capacity to live *in* this world wholly centred upon God. In union, you will be intermittently conscious of the overwhelming reality of God, or rather you will be aware of a sort of overpowering 'blankness' of ideas and feelings, a sense of immensity beyond everything ('all the faculties are lost',[4] she says, all particular sensations and thoughts fall away); but meanwhile, you go on your way doing calmly and effectively what is required of you.

But Teresa goes beyond John of the Cross in at least three respects. First, she provides a far more detailed analysis of the kinds of things that may be experienced in the transitional times, a catalogue of extraordinary phenomena, and gives practical advice about discerning the important from the unimportant and the true from the false. Both in *The Book of My Life* and in *Interior Castle*, she speaks from her own experience and the experience of advising countless others. Her analysis of different kinds of vision, for example, is one of the most valuable discussions in the whole of Christian spiritual literature.

Second, she insists, very boldly and in full consciousness, that she is going against a lot of received wisdom, that you must never deliberately stop reflecting on the incarnate person of Jesus. Others had written that a stage comes when you are directly in touch with the heavenly Christ, the eternal Son – or at least that you should move beyond meditation on the incarnate life. Teresa, especially in the sixth section of *Interior Castle*, daringly says that people who give such advice don't really understand what is going on in themselves. No one comes to the Father but through Jesus, after all, and we are not angels but people living in mortal bodies. So we need to be in touch with the *bodily* life of Jesus.

Now of course there will be times when we cannot engage in formal meditation in the strict sense, orderly reflection with the intellect; sometimes God just makes this impossible. She would not, I think, disagree with John of the Cross and others that there come times when it is indeed inappropriate to use deliberate mental exercises when God wants to give us something deeper. But there are more informal ways of thinking about Jesus, says Teresa: there is the 'simple gaze' at an image of the passion, an unsystematic absorption in some bit of the gospel story – and, as she says here and elsewhere, there is the loving gaze we direct to Christ in the Sacrament, which is the sign of Jesus' willingness to be there for us daily and continuously. To turn away from all this is fatal to our discipleship. Teresa even advises us to have to hand a picture of Jesus to take out and look at from time to time, just to remind us of the absolute centrality of the incarnate life.

Third, Teresa repeats many times that in the state of union 'Mary and Martha join to welcome Jesus'.[5] The

condition we grow towards is one in which contemplation and action are inseparable. Being Christian is *one*
thing: being present in the world with God at the centre of all your experience. *From* that hidden centre, the
'mission' of God goes forward in the acts and words of
your life. Contemplation is the steady learning of how
to turn towards that centre, which is at the same time
a turning to the world God loves. In other words, our
own Christian lives are themselves a pattern of incarnation, of coming *into* the present moment so that it
becomes transparent to God. While we are still growing
into the fullness of this, there will be times of acute
anguish, when we wish we were away from it all, 'safe
in the arms of Jesus', but the great breakthrough comes
when we no longer want to be anywhere but where we
are and let God work through our engagement with the
here and now. We have at last become attuned to God,
contemplation has become second nature, and our lives
communicate the divine act. There is no longer a gap
between Mary and Martha.

So we come back to where we began. Teresa's whole
life and the witness of her communities of friendship
and simplicity is a lived theology, and a theology of
incarnation. Teresa was not a social campaigner or a
politician, but what she offered was simply another

model of life together, grounded in the gift of God's welcome and the daily attempt to keep our own hearts open to this in silence and adoration. In such a life, we may learn as she did to see *through* the anxieties of the social world to a shared human kinship cemented in the identification of God the Son with our human condition. Our own society is, if anything, becoming more, not less, like Teresa's fearful, bitter and prejudiced environment. What are we going to learn of prayer and common life from this Doctor of the Church that will address the unhappiness and inhumanity of our own time?

John Milton

1608–74

From heroism to fidelity

To begin with a resoundingly obvious remark: John Milton believed profoundly in words. He worked out of a pervasive confidence that his language could sound the depths of truth and communicate them in such a way as to change human hearts. In his long writing life, he found very diverse ways of expressing this. Beginning with the musical, extravagant idioms of his earliest poems with their rich classical allusiveness and dancing rhythms, he went on to establish himself as a prose polemicist of immense – sometimes scurrilous – vigour, and wrote what is probably the greatest apologia in any European language for free debate in the public arena. He became a servant of the government, using his skills for the wholesale reformation of a society. And then, already shaken by personal and political disaster and by his irreversible blindness, he embarked on the most ambitious project of all, 'to justify the ways of God to man': in a startlingly different poetic style, severe, insistent, but with even more metaphorical abundance than before, he dramatized the fall of the angels, the inner counsels of the Trinity and the first disobedience of the human heart.

His whole life rested on the presumption that words rightly used could both capture all that could be understood and change what was possible for human beings. Like any great poet, he was not afraid of risks; and some of them do and some of them don't come off. Even C. S. Lewis, one of his finest and most sympathetic twentieth-century interpreters, notes that Milton's heaven is too close for comfort to Homer's Olympus: the unimaginable and transcendent trinitarian God of orthodox Christianity metamorphoses into a committee of ceremonious potentates. Yet Milton would undoubtedly have argued in his defence that if you're going to imagine, you have to imagine boldly: of course it isn't like that in heaven, but how else does language have access, the access it needs, to the mysterious if you shrink away from the task of redeeming the idioms of mythology?

But – again like any great poet – he moves inexorably towards the moment where it becomes plain that music, sonority and symbolic abundance still leave something uncaptured, and even the most disciplined of metrical schemes only exposes something that cannot be reduced to metre or measure. George Herbert acknowledges it

in a number of extraordinary poems where he deliberately interrupts the flow of rhythm with silence – as in
'The Sacrifice' – or with a line beyond 'measure, tune
and time' – as in 'Grief'.

Milton, more intensely ambitious and surely less self-
aware than Herbert, struggles with this. There is a kind
of prophetic foretaste of it in the well-known Sonnet
XIX, 'When I consider how my light is spent', as early
as the 1650s, with its conclusion, 'They also serve who
only stand and wait'. Here he has to accept the limita-
tion of what he can do as a blind man, and this leads
to a reluctant but still, in literary terms, authoritative
commendation of patience and stillness. Yet he continues to be ambitious for what he can say; *Paradise Lost*
makes that as evident as could be. What happens when
it is no longer clear even what can be said?

At the very end of *Paradise Lost*, the archangel Michael
has laid out before the newly fallen Adam what lies
ahead: the glorious history of God's dealings with his
people, up to and including the restoration of human-
kind in Christ. Adam responds with a foreshadowing
of the Easter Vigil proclamation of the Catholic Church:

Full of doubt I stand,
Whether I should repent me now of sin,

> By me done, and occasion'd; or rejoice
> Much more, that much more good thereof shall spring.[1]

The long-term future is assured, and Adam knows that a 'greater Man' will restore all things.[2] And yet, when the dialogue with the archangel is over and Adam and Eve leave Paradise, 'They hand in hand, with wandering steps and slow, Through Eden took their solitary way.'[3] These final lines of *Paradise Lost* have an immense poignancy and sense of desolation. The reconciled future is known, but it is a long journey to arrive at it. The interval is a time of disorientation, loss and loneliness, and there are no short cuts.

Adam stands; he stands and waits, not knowing how to bring together in words the appalling gravity of his loss and the excess of glory promised for his descendants. It is not a vision that can be simply articulated so that appropriate feelings are guaranteed; he and Eve must now begin their journey – walking both away from and towards bliss and reconciliation; and the words left to them are the words they will have to find on this journey as they walk it. When Adam rejoins Eve after Michael's prophecies, and she tells him that she has received the same message in her dreams, Adam (uncharacteristically) 'answer'd not'.[4] He leaves Paradise in silence. The vision is given that will give Adam and Eve the resource to walk down the precipitous slopes of Eden to middle earth, but the words are not yet there to hold it all together.

It is a glimpse of the complex challenges that run through the last poems Milton wrote. *Paradise Regain'd* is emotionally dominated by Satan's frustration at the unrevealing nature of his encounters with Jesus in the wilderness. He cannot identify what it is that Jesus actually wants – and, to a large extent, neither can we. The old Milton, who could confidently depict the persons of the Trinity discussing the salvation of the world, is still in evidence, of course: we are treated to a soliloquy from Jesus about his childhood and his present uncertainty as to what lies ahead. And Jesus' repudiation of Satan's offer of universal power and popularity has the authentic Miltonic note of angry contempt for a fickle and stupid general public; rather more Miltonic than biblical.

But the climax is strikingly austere. When Satan has placed Jesus on the pinnacle of the Temple, he:

> added thus in scorn;
> There stand, if thou wilt stand; to stand upright
> Will ask thee skill . . .

> Now shew thy Progeny; if not to stand,
> Cast thy self down.[5]

The response is devastatingly brief:

> To whom thus Jesus: also it is written,
> Tempt not the Lord thy God, he said and stood.[6]

Like Adam, Jesus stands. The fact that he does is the final answer to Satan, who, witnessing Jesus standing in triumphant silence, promptly falls. Milton's analogy is significant. Satan falls as did the Sphinx who asked the fatal riddle at the crossroads in Greek mythology; when Oedipus answered the riddle correctly, the Sphinx 'Cast herself headlong from the Ismenian steep'.[7] Jesus stands and answers Satan's riddles and, as with Oedipus and the Sphinx, the answer is a definition of humanity itself. But this definition is of a humanity anchored immovably in God: the final and true definition of our life is revealed in the figure who alone is able to stand upright on the dangerous summit of the Temple, between heaven and earth.

The words of Jesus' response lack any of the rhetorical elaboration that attends his earlier replies to Satan. What matters, we might say, is that Jesus holds his place between earth and heaven, native to both. Speech gives way to a bare act of witness; Milton's earlier language in the sonnet is given a far deeper anchorage here. And the answer to Jesus' own self-questioning as well as to Satan's obsessive attempt to discover what Jesus wants and what he will do is made plain. Whatever Jesus says or does, he will 'stand'; his fidelity is part of what he is, unshakeably, as his freedom is inseparably bound up with his obedience. His speech moves into this sheer victorious presence.

The odd unsatisfactoriness of *Paradise Regain'd* in the eyes of many readers is as much as anything to do with this climax, poetically surprising and morally challenging. Milton himself did not exactly leave things there. *Samson Agonistes* is, more than anything else Milton wrote, marked by irregular rhythms, awkward changes of metre and fractured lines, as if finally yielding to what Herbert had seen – that the realities with which poetry deals cannot be contained in polished and smooth forms. Yet the narrative is troubling, with its bloody and vengeful denouement. Samson, rather than 'standing' in witness to God's inscrutable justice, becomes the agent of divine judgement through mass slaughter.

Yet *Paradise Regain'd* still 'stands'. That moment of triumph and stillness is as far as Milton ever got in declaring the nature both of poetry itself and of God's saving action. Poetry, when it is fully itself, enacts something of the cross and resurrection, abandoning its

fluencies and successes in order to press further and
further towards that 'thin' texture through which truth
may perhaps come. Poets, like Prospero at the end of
The Tempest, have to know when to drown their books,
when to let go of the defences of rhetoric and the illu-
sions of fully controlling what they say. Milton trusted
language perhaps more than most poets and polemicists,
and much could be said about the cost of his 'letting
go', both personally and poetically.

It is hard to guess just how much he was enabled to
confront it by a faith that insists that abandonment and
an undressed, unforced language is God's own idiom for
making himself known: the word of the cross, as St Paul
calls it. God saves not by heroic acts – not through a
Samson – but by being who he is: by a human life and
death that simply fleshes out God's own fidelity to himself:

> whatever place,
> Habit, or state, or motion, still expressing
> The Son of God.[8]

The poet cannot finally avoid the summons from con-
fident speech to the brokenness and harsh linguistic
economy of witness; the disciple cannot avoid the summons from heroism to silent fidelity, knowing only that
this has been God's way of transforming the world. 'If

we have died with Christ, we believe that we will also live with him' (Romans 6.8). Milton, poet and disciple, faces this as reluctantly as any great or heroic figure ever did. Yet face it he does – patchily and reluctantly, but truthfully; and so must we.

A sermon preached on Wednesday 17 September 2008 at St Giles Cripplegate, London, at a service to celebrate the 400th anniversary of the birth of the poet John Milton.

William Wilberforce
1759–1833
The moral state

I was once invited by a national newspaper to name the most influential British citizen of the last millennium. I didn't have much hesitation: it is not easy to think of anyone other than Wilberforce whose legacy affected the lives of so many millions yet whose struggle against inhumanity enjoyed so little in the way of financial or military support. So much rested on the personal motivation of one man, encouraged by a small and dedicated group.

This is not to minimize the contribution of those others who offered support, nor is it to overlook the importance of slaves and former slaves themselves in the struggle, including those who led slave revolts in the colonies and so brought the urgency of the issue before the eyes of so many. But there was one specific bit of business to do – a process in the legislature of the United Kingdom – and that business was accomplished by William Wilberforce.

Perhaps predictably, there have been attempts to minimize or relativize his achievement or to make us think just a little less of him. In Wilberforce's own life-time, William Cobbett kept up a fairly steady stream of belittling criticism, suggesting that the MP for Hull was more concerned about slaves in distant countries than about the poor on his doorstep. More recently, the same evangelical Christianity that fired his passion for aboli-tion has been quoted in reproach. He was more inter-ested in souls than bodies, some have said, caring more about the spread of the gospel than about abolition in itself, even regarding slavery as a providential for Africans to be converted to Christianity.

But it is a serious mistake to suppose that Wilberforce should be judged guilty of covert racism or sympathy with slavery on the grounds that he believed Christianity had brought advantages to slaves. And it is undeniable that Christianity acted as an engine of criticism, not of compliance, for so many who lived in slavery, in the eighteenth century and after. But this raises a substan-tial issue with extensive bearing on how we are to judge the lasting elements of Wilberforce's legacy.

The issue is this: apart from Christianity, what were or what could have been the factors that could drive any critique of slavery in the eighteenth century? We think of the Age of Enlightenment as an intellectual climate in which the assumptions of modern liberal and democratic thought were first formed, and that is not wholly wrong. But we will look in vain to the secularizing writers of the period for systematic criticisms of slavery, let alone campaigns for its ending. The liberal and egalitarian principles of the French Enlightenment made not the slightest dent upon the slave system (and the post-Revolution French administrations made no move towards emancipation of their own accord). The egalitarianism of the age was like that of the Stoics in ancient Rome – a theory for the elite, unrelated to actual human relationships in the present, where, sadly but conveniently, primitive justice and equality had been rendered unattainable. And we must not forget the ways in which some aspects of enlightened thinking could end up *reinforcing* attitudes of racial superiority by appeal to the normative status of European thinking and the assumption that non-Europeans were incapable of 'standard' reasoning.

What is it that moves egalitarianism from being a wistful theory to being the motive for serious political action? The answer is very simple: the conviction of responsibility before God. Wilberforce and his circle were bound by that conviction; they believed that if a sinful system existed and its sinfulness implicated them as well as others, they were under an obligation to end it. God could not will sin, so if there were sin in the political and economic conditions under which they pursued their business, it was God's will that it be eradicated. There is no place here for wistfulness or for a 'tragic' sense of unavoidable moral compromise. We may think this, as a principle, worryingly naive, but what is undeniable is that it motivated a series of major social changes, not only in respect of slavery.

It was one of Wilberforce's most powerful insights – as it was of St Augustine many centuries earlier – that injustice damages the oppressor spiritually as much as it damages the oppressed materially. If there is a recognizable 'Enlightenment' strain in Wilberforce's thinking, it is that of a Christian enlightened self-interest: an unjust and unlawful system may bring profit in the short term but it injures and destroys souls in the long term. This is not to reduce the abolitionist passion to a refined selfishness – we have only to read what Christian abolitionists wrote to see the strength of their plain abhorrence of the cruelties involved. But it is a significant element in any such moral campaign to ask about the effect of immorality on the health of the individual's soul, to make the oppressor grasp that their own humanity is fatally compromised by the oppressive relationship, and that in God's eyes they will have to give account of how they undermined that humanity in themselves.

Understanding this point should help us see one of the central aspects of Wilberforce's legacy. There is no simple gulf between personal and public morality, and Christian morality is not about 'keeping yourself unspotted from the world' in any sense that simply implies withdrawing or ignoring public wrongs. In a democratic state – even one as imperfectly democratic as eighteenth- and early nineteenth-century Britain – the citizen is morally involved in what the state actively enables or supports in terms of the common life.

Put like that, the legacy may seem alarming to some. Does it not lend itself to a politics of relentless pressure-group activity, lobbying and perhaps even imposing standards of moral behaviour on non-believers? Wilberforce and his circle, we should note, were deeply preoccupied with personal morality, but they did not seek to enforce purely personal morality by public legislation. Responsibility to God was not for them the same thing as responsibility before the law of the land – nor would we expect it to be, since they lay such emphasis on the believer's free decision to obey God's law. The campaign for the reform of 'Public Manners', with which Wilberforce and the 'Clapham Sect' were so closely associated, was about confronting the ethos and assumptions of a culture, but not about imposing morality by statute. Personal morality is precisely that – an area where individuals are free and able to make the decisions that shape their own particular lives.

But if the state enacts or perpetuates in the corporate life of the nation what is directly contrary to the Christian understanding of God's purpose for humanity – if it endorses slavery, for example – the Christian is bound to protest and to argue in the public sphere for change, through whatever channels are available. This is something that implicates every citizen, irrespective of his or her personal choices. There is a difference between matters of personal choice and those other matters which, because they help to determine the economy of a whole society, involve everyone who benefits from that economy. So Christian activism in respect of changing the law is justified primarily when the state is responsible for – so to speak   compromising the morality of all its citizens. In such a situation, the state is in effect limiting the freedom of its own citizens by involving them in the consequences of morally questionable actions.

This, I suggest, is at the heart of what Wilberforce was concerned about. He was not campaigning for the state to impose a personal morality, and would probably, if this were put to him in such terms, have agreed that such a policy would take away the essential aspect of personal liberty in choices about one's own life. But he *was* campaigning for a moral state – that is, for a state that does not compromise its citizens, and that recognizes its own accountability to considerations wider than those of immediate profit and security. He wanted the government to understand that its policies directly shaped the moral status of citizens: public policy creates the world in which particular citizens live their lives; it creates a climate, a set of possibilities, a language and culture of public life or international life. And this moulds what is possible for individuals; it does not – obviously – mean that they are directly and simply responsible for things they have not chosen, but it does mean that the horizons of their moral vision, or at least their practical possibilities, are limited. The public climate has the capacity to make people less than they might be.

If we accept that public morality is inseparably connected with the moral health and well-being of persons in a society and that human moral agents can be damaged by being implicated in public and corporate immorality, we are in effect saying that the state's organs of action cannot be immune from challenge on moral grounds. In the absence of a universally shared and assumed moral and religious system, this challenging will be a matter of mobilizing and motivating the public at large to bring pressure to bear on public authority because that general public has caught a vision (the Jubilee 2000 campaign, for example, and also the beginnings of consumer pressure around ecological matters as it begins to spill over into political pressure). For that to happen, what I have called communities of moral tradition need to go on developing their self-awareness and self-confidence in areas of collective moral issues (not to confuse this with ill-fated and ill-focused campaigns on questions of personal morality, which are not sensibly addressed through legislative processes).

Wilberforce believed politics was a vocation because he saw politics as always opening out beyond itself. Good politics was in significant part a matter of trying to make sure that a state's public policy did not compromise the souls of its citizens, clouding and complicating their responsibility before God. It is a powerful and a crucial legacy. Our democracy is very different now from what it was in 1806, but some of the dangers are much the same. And Wilberforce confronts us now with the

question, 'If Christians, committed to personal responsibility and social justice, cannot keep before the eyes
of the state and its legislators issues that are greater than
security and profit, who can?'

*From an address given on 24 April 2007 at the invitation
of the Wilberforce Lecture Trust, at the City Hall in Hull.*

Charles Dickens

1812–70

The truth of exaggeration

It's difficult to tell the truth about human beings. Every novelist knows this in a special way, and when Dickens sets out to tell the truth about human beings he does it outrageously, by exaggeration, by caricature. The figures we remember most readily from his works are the great grotesques. We have, we think, never met anyone like them. And then we think again.

The truth is extreme; the truth is excessive. The truth about human beings is more grotesque and bizarre than we can imagine. And Dickens' generous embrace of human beings does not arise out of a chilly sense of what is due to them, but out of a celebratory feeling that there is always more to be discovered in them. Even his villains are exuberant. It was George Orwell who pointed out that when Mr Murdstone sets David Copperfield one of those appalling sums in his unhappy childhood, it is couched in terms of calculating a certain number of Double Gloucester cheeses. Orwell points out that a real Murdstone would never have thought of the cheeses: it's part of that overflow, that unnecessary, excessive sense of what is human, that takes us from page to page in Dickens, eyebrows raised and breath bated.

Dickens is the enemy not so much of an unjust view of human beings as of a *boring* view of human beings. He loved the poor and the destitute, not so much from a sense of duty as from a sense of outrage that their lives were being made flat and dead. He wanted them to live. He wanted them to expand into the space that should be available for human beings to be what God meant them to be. In *Hard Times*, he left us one of the most unforgettable pictures of what education looks like if it forgets that exuberance and excess, and treats human beings as small containers for information and skill.

And that sense of the grotesque is, strange as it may sound to say it, one of the things that makes Dickens a great religious writer. As is clear from *The Life of Our Lord*, he could write simply and movingly about Christ. He could, in *A Christmas Carol*, leave us one of the greatest modern myths to arise out of the Christian story. But he had relatively little time for conventional religion, and no time at all for those who substituted conventional religion for that exuberant celebration of the human which he was interested in.

> Mr Chadbands he wos a prayin wunst at Mr Sangsby's
> and I heerd him, but he sounded as if he wos a-speakin'
> to hisself, and not to me. He prayed a lot, but I couldn't
> make out nothink on it.[1]

The Chadbands and the Jellybys and all those other unforgettably exuberant hypocrites in his books: these are the people on whom, at the end of the day, Dickens wishes judgement to be passed.

But that sense of excess in the human spirit and the human heart also leads on to another side of Dickens, equally serious, equally religious, much more disturbing: the side of Dickens that makes him indeed a novelist to stand alongside the very greatest imaginative spirits in Europe – and this is Dickens' sense of the tragic. Dickens writes about people in hell, and he knows what hell is like. He describes people in the hell of concealment, deceit and self-deceit – William Dorrit, Mr Merdle, Lady Dedlock people who cannot live, literally, when their myths about themselves are destroyed. Part of this sense of exuberance in Dickens is the recognition that all of us live by projecting myths and dramas about ourselves. We tell stories about ourselves, we write scripts for ourselves and we love to act them out.

But what happens when those stories and those scripts are so far from reality that we cannot actually survive the touch of truth? Tragedy in Dickens is so often about that appalling moment when a myth is shattered, and a person with it. And along with the hell of deceit and of self-deceit, there are the hells of obsession – of Mr Monks and Miss Havisham, Mrs Clennam and Bradley Headstone, people who have lost all their freedom and are strangers to humane Dickensian exuberance because they have been taken prisoner by something in themselves, locking them in, weighing them down. They are part of Dickens' unparalleled portraiture of self-destruction.

Perhaps these depictions of hell – the hells of self-deceit and obsession and self-destruction – owed something to Dickens' own painful self-awareness. He was a man who recognized the gaps in his own life between aspiration and reality, public myth and private shame; a man who in his own exuberance drove himself towards self-destruction – and yet in that very process drew out extraordinary levels of sheer joy and festive celebratory hearing of what he had to say.

A man, then, who portrays human beings excessively and extravagantly, a man who portrays human beings in hell; and yet, when we read him, it does not read like bad news. What does he have to say at the end of the day about redemption? In some ways, not a great deal. Or, rather, there is a tension again and again in his books between a carefully, neatly resolved, happy ending and an immense burden of recognized, almost unbearable, unresolved suffering.

He achieves the balance most perfectly (for this reader, anyway) in *Bleak House*, where the past tense of Esther's narrative is balanced by the present tense of unhealed suffering, the rain still falling on the Lincolnshire Wolds. But in that book also we have one of the strangest, most startling images that he ever gives us of compassion and mercy, and that is the figure of Sir Leicester Dedlock. At the very end of *Bleak House*, left alone in his decaying mansion, holding open the possibility of forgiveness and restoration, 'I revoke no dispositions I have made in her favour,' says Sir Leicester, with his typical, apparently passionless, precision about the wife who has fled from him in guilt and terror.[2] And in that appallingly stiff phrase we hear something of the hope of mercy: almost silent, powerless, Sir Leicester after his stroke, dying slowly in loneliness, stubbornly holds open the possibility that there might be, once again, love and harmony.

'We may confidently hope that God will forgive us our sins and mistakes, and enable us to live and die in peace,' says Dickens for his children.[3] And perhaps for us as grown-ups (or people who might quite like to be grown-ups one day), the image of the hope of God's forgiveness is expressed in its most shocking vividness in that lonely figure stubbornly holding the door open, revoking no dispositions made in our favour. Powerless to enforce love or justice, and yet indestructibly, even extravagantly, offering the only kind of love that is appropriate to the extravagant and excessive nature of human beings. An utterly unreasonable compassion, which, because of its utter unreasonableness, can change everything.

An address given on 7 February 2012 at the Wreath-laying Ceremony in Westminster Abbey, marking the bicentenary of the birth of Charles Dickens.

Florence Nightingale

1820–1910

The light of life

Florence Nightingale may very aptly be described as a luminary: somebody who literally brought light into dark places. But she was somebody who was also able to name with precision, with illuminating exactitude, the need and the suffering that was there before her, who was able to see what others couldn't see or refused to see; somebody who, in lifting her eyes to eternal love, at the same time focused her eyes on earthly suffering. It's quite a balancing act, and the extraordinary character of Florence Nightingale lies very much in the way she held that balance.

She reminds us all – as she reminded Victorian society – that love needs clear sight, that it isn't enough to say the right things, to make general sympathetic noises. Love, if it is going to make a difference, has to be precise. And that is why the nursing training, the professional tradition that derives from her, is not simply a training in nursing skills but also a training in seeing clearly. A trained nurse, in Florence Nightingale's vision, was somebody who could see, who was educated to see the particular, not to gloss it over, not to make it easy, but to see it as God sees the numberless stars – each face unique, each name special – and out of that to see what the needs are that love must serve.

It's often said that it's very easy to love humanity – the problem is human beings. And to love with clarity means, of course, to love human beings in their particularity and to cast light on individuals, the particular needs of this person, this patient; not to generalize but to attend, to look. Lift your eyes to the heavens, because that's the only way of focusing them on earth. Lift your eyes to endless, exact, intelligent love, the love that sustains everything – and something of that intelligent love will spill over into your own care, into your own devotion and attention.

But, of course, that is as much as to say that caring changes us. Caring is not simply something we do: put on, put off, switch on, switch off. It changes us as people. And one of the hardest challenges for those in the 'caring' professions is to know how to cope with that in ways that are not invasive and crippling or crushing; to let the reality of what is there change them and not to let it devour them.

So caring is about clear vision, realism, the clear sight of what's there, the refusal to turn away from the particular to the general; and because of that it's also about being changed in the encounter, having your heart and your mind stretched, growing up in and through the business of caring, in and through the encounter with suffering. All of this is part of Florence Nightingale's legacy. She was certainly changed by her encounter with suffering; she was a person who was in many ways a good example of the cost that comes with honest engagement.

She was in many ways a phenomenally difficult woman – obstinate, self-righteous, generous, sacrificial, angular, judgemental and compassionate all at once, so much changed by the encounter with suffering that her life showed cost, damage even. The risks were real, and they still are. And yet in allowing herself to be changed, to be in some ways almost moulded out of shape by the suffering she encountered, she made a difference that no one else could have made.

We can't any of us plan to be obnoxious, angular and difficult – mostly we just are by nature. We can't plan to be difficult and unique saints. We manage normally to be rather average sinners. But we can look at someone like Florence Nightingale and think of the cost of attention. What did it cost her to see clearly, exactly, to see the specifics? How did it change her? Only because it changed *her* did it change the face of nursing care in Britain and far more widely. It may give us, of course, a little bit of patience with ourselves and one another, recognizing that sometimes things are only changed when they become more, not less, difficult. But, above all, she ought to remind us that it is quite simply possible, if your eyes are fixed on an uncompromising love, to see more clearly and then to love more exactly; possible to be changed, and changed in such a way that everything is changed around you.

We speak often of the saints as burning and shining lights in their generation. And, as we all know, that is an image very much at the heart of the mythology of 'the Lady with the Lamp'. But for all of us who seek to follow the calling of care, something of the same applies. We are all called to enlighten, to provide a perspective that will allow things to be seen clearly; we are all called to give that focused, specific attention that begins to give light to those most deeply in darkness because they feel they've been forgotten and never attended to.

We talk perhaps less often than we used to about nursing as a vocation. And that's a pity, because a calling of any kind is a calling to be changed – it is not just a calling to do a job but a calling to grow into a certain kind of humanity. And generations upon generations of nurses responded to that call because – as much as anything – they wanted to be a certain kind of human being.

I hope that the nursing profession continues to be something that calls people who want to be a certain kind of human being, not just to do a job, not just to write things on lists, not just to contribute to some analysis of productivity and efficiency, but to be a particular kind of person, to be someone who sees with precision, who attends to the particular, and, in all of that, who risks being changed; not just caring from outside but being alongside; negotiating the great difficulties that brings; keeping your own space, your own integrity and your own freedom, yet at the same time being generously open. No one pretends that that is easy. But when it happens, when people do grow into that kind of humanity, things change. Light shines in dark places, other people's eyes are lifted and they discover something of that extraordinary promise in the book of Isaiah: 'They shall mount up on wings like eagles. They shall run and not grow weary' (Isaiah 40.31).

Florence Nightingale, like many other reformers, ran fast and furiously to achieve her ends, and she didn't always mind very much whom she elbowed out of the way in the process either. But, with that eagle eye of hers, she saw what needed to be done and she did it; she saw because she was changed by the love to which day after day she lifted her eyes.

A sermon preached on 15 May 2010 in the chapel of St Thomas' Hospital, marking the 100th anniversary of the death of Florence Nightingale.

Sergei Bulgakov

1871–1944

Politics, art and prayer

For most of continental Europe, the twentieth century was a nightmare era. Those of us who have grown up in other parts of the world probably still don't quite understand what the corporate trauma of twentieth-century Europe meant to so many. Millions of people in Europe lived through the end of their world; millions lived through it not once but twice: in the tearing up of the map of Europe that followed the First World War, and in the massive displacements as well as the unspeakable suffering and slaughter that characterized the Second World War and the years immediately afterwards.

It's a history that makes the beginnings of Christianity somehow more intelligible, closer than we might have thought. Jesus' preaching and the first witness of the early Christians took place in a world where the end of all things was expected. And a great deal of what Jesus taught was about how to live through the end of the world, when all that you consider to be familiar, controllable and reliable disappears. So it is hardly surprising that so many figures of spiritual and intellectual stature and complexity in the twentieth century discovered or rediscovered Christian faith at a completely new level of depth as they lived through the ends of their worlds.

Sergei Bulgakov grew up in the late nineteenth century in a priest's family in rural Russia. In his autobiography he describes the climate of the parsonage in which he grew up: a father with a bit of a drink problem who earned most of his income as chaplain to the cemetery, which meant that his pastoral duties were in some ways occasional and rather limited; a mother desperately overworked, nerve-ridden, tense and perpetually worried about money. He didn't find anything in the religion of his childhood that held his interest and allegiance, and in his teenage years, after a couple of years in seminary, his faith disappeared. He became a radical, a Marxist, and made such a success of his career as an economist that, in the last decade of the nineteenth century and the beginning of the twentieth, many people regarded him as the great rising hope of intellectual Marxism in Russia. Lenin thought of the young Bulgakov with respect as one of the great theorists of the Marxist future.

It's not completely clear what made the difference, but around 1903 the young Dr Bulgakov, fresh from the publication of a massive work on the application of Marxist theory to agriculture, decided that Marxism wasn't quite enough. He began to read novelists and philosophers from outside his own world. He read Dostoevsky seriously, he studied Nietzsche and Hegel, and he even began to read some nineteenth-century English biblical scholarship (which he rather admired). Slowly, he found his way back to Christian belief.

He decided to stand for election to the second democratic assembly in Russia in 1907 as a Christian Socialist, but found that a year of active politics (including being briefly the equivalent of an MP for a Christian socialist party) left him angry, disillusioned and frustrated. He wrote some more books; one of his children died tragically young; and then he was removed from his post at the university in Moscow, partly because of his subversive ideas, partly because of economic cutbacks in the university. With impeccable timing, he offered himself for ordination in 1917. After the Revolution, he was exiled and spent the rest of his life in Paris, where he was the founder and first principal of a very famous Russian theological college in Paris – St Serge. He died in 1944.

It was a life that spanned a very great deal of the end of the European world, in more than one way. He had already in 1903 seen through to the end of the Marxist revolution: he wrote an essay in the first decade of the twentieth century in which he lays out the fatal structural weaknesses in the Marxist approach to humanity. In the 1980s, essays like this were secretly reprinted, passed from hand to hand in the Soviet Union, and read, rightly, as prophetic of the collapse of the system that was just beginning to come on to the scene in Bulgakov's early professional career. He saw that there was more to politics than politics, and among his most interesting work in the first decade of the century is a reflection on the interweaving of politics, art and liturgy as three ways in which human beings transform the world they're in: *politics*, which seeks to transform the relationships between people and between social groups; *art*, which seeks to transform the material stuff of the world; and *liturgy*, in which human beings invite God to transform the entire environment in which they live – inner and outer.

And he insists that each one of these dries and withers without the others. A politics that's only politics ends up in managerial tyranny or worse: he knew about that and could see where the politics of his day was going. Art for art's sake leaves you with a lot of highly cultivated dilettantes who never really make a difference to anything. Liturgy without politics and art isolates the vital presence of the body of Christ in the midst of the world from the real concerns of human beings. But bring them all together and you understand what the Church is: the Church, the community of the new creation, the new reality in which the political, the creative and the devotional/spiritual are absolutely fused together so that there is something utterly new.

Bulgakov is an endlessly fascinating and inspiring figure. I include him among my luminaries because this is a life *making sense*, in that he was someone who saw through to the end of some of the great temptations and seductions of his day and took the immensely risky step of trying to find a way of living that holds together, in thought and prayer and action, the range and depth of the new creation.

In his last years he had an enormous reputation as a spiritual director, and I imagine that the ghost of the young Marxist intellectual must have given a wry smile to see the older Bulgakov acting as a deeply loved and revered spiritual guide in Paris in exile. And it was some of those people whom he directed spiritually who, visiting him on his deathbed, spoke about the light that they saw in his face – more than just a reflected light, they all said. In the last few weeks after a stroke that left him incapable of speaking, people would go into his darkened room and find there was light emanating from his face.

Bulgakov himself would have said, as would many Orthodox theologians, that one of the things that the saints do is (literally and metaphorically) to 'shed light', to make sense – by challenging, stepping out of some of the prisons that human beings shut themselves into, making sense by seeking a way of discipleship where the wholeness of new creation can come alive.

From an address given on 5 June 2008 to the Hereford Diocesan Conference.

Edith Stein

1891–1942

Thinking in solidarity

The life of Edith Stein is another twentieth-century European story of disruption, risk and profound suffering. She came from a Jewish family, not particularly practising, but with some religious background. She studied philosophy and became a very distinguished teacher of philosophy and the trusted associate of one of the most important German philosophers of the day. But as her philosophical imagination deepened and developed, she found that there were questions she could no longer avoid. She couldn't stop herself thinking about what it was within and beyond the world of phenomena that made sense of love and sacrifice and devotion (she had written a graduate thesis on the concept of empathy, one of the first and still one of the most important and original essays on the topic).

For a time she left her academic work to nurse casualties of the First World War. At last, having been overwhelmed by reading some of the work of St Teresa of Avila, to the immense surprise (indeed, dismay) of many of her family and her professional associates, she decided to become a Roman Catholic and a Carmelite nun. She took the habit as Sr Teresa Benedicta of the Cross and became an enclosed contemplative. In the convent she still worked on philosophy, but now with a new focus. Among her concerns was the frontier territory between philosophy and mysticism, and she wrote a very difficult but extremely important book on St John of the Cross, the great sixteenth-century Spanish Carmelite mystic.

Whether she expected to live out her days in the Carmelite convent in relative peace, I don't know. She was a wise woman and could read the signs of the times as well as anybody else could. She was relocated from Germany to Holland as the Third Reich tightened its grip on Germany. When the Germans invaded Holland and rounded up those who had previously fled from Germany, they were particularly interested in those of Jewish background. The Dutch Catholic bishops issued a strong protest about the treatment of the Jews and, in reprisal, Christians of Jewish families were sought out. Sr Teresa Benedicta was arrested as a Jew, and she died in Auschwitz. She was canonized by Pope John Paul II in 1998.

Three important things emerge in her story. One is obviously that here is somebody – as with Bulgakov – entering deeply into the mind and imagination of her

own time. She was very near the heart of the philosophical revolution that was going on in German uni-
versities in the early twentieth century and, going right
to the boundaries of what people were thinking and
imagining, found herself almost irresistibly drawn over
the edge. It's as if, when you look deeply enough into
politics (like Bulgakov) or philosophy (like Edith Stein),
you're at considerable risk of falling over this edge. Go
far enough with the disciplines of this world in hon-
esty and integrity, and God is waiting for you.

But I also think of two more poignant elements of
her life. She was somebody who moved from Judaism
to Christianity – an appallingly difficult thing to do –
yet she died because she was a Jew and because she
would not conceal or compromise that fact. She was
quite explicit that she was ready to die with her fellow
Jews. She was not eager to leave Germany – she wanted
to share the reproach of her people (an allusion there,
I think, to Psalm 69) – but she had no choice; she was
moved by her order. But it was as a Jew that she died,
accepting the catastrophe of her people, sharing the
suffering of those most deeply vulnerable and at risk
because of their Jewishness in the world of that time.
That's one of the ways in which she *made sense* of the
nightmare of Germany in the 1930s. Yes, she was a

Christian and she believed the Christian faith to be true, but she knew that her discipleship would not allow her to put a safe distance between her and her people who were suffering; would not allow her to modify or play down the call of God to be where the weak and the suffering were.

So she accepted that risk and died because of it. But she also knew that the conflict in Germany in the 1930s was about more than politics: it was about 'who is Lord'. Just as in the early church the martyrs died because they would not say 'Caesar is Lord' (they knew that this was what Jesus was), so with Edith Stein. One of the most vivid stories I know about her is about the moment of her arrest, when she was summoned to the convent parlour by the SS commandant who was rounding up the Jews in the area. He greeted her with the words '*Heil, Hitler*', and she greeted him with what she said to her sisters every morning of her life: '*Laudetur Jesus Christus*' ('Jesus Christ be praised'). There, you might say, are the two lordships in conflict in the 1930s; her response was once again in the form of a life making sense of a sense-less and terrible world.

We catch a glimpse of her on the transports to Auschwitz in an extraordinary little vignette written by another great figure of the time: a young Jewish woman from Amsterdam called Etty Hillesum, whose letters and diaries have been published in recent years. Etty Hillesum, writing to her sister from Westerbork (the transit camp where the Jews were being sent off to Auschwitz), says that she has just met two German nuns who are being sent to the camp because of their Jewishness. 'What an extraordinary impact they made,' she says, 'on those who met them even just for a few moments in the train.' One of those was Edith Stein, the other her sister, Rose. Etty Hillesum died in Auschwitz, along with Edith Stein and others.

How do we *make sense* of these stories? Only by telling them over again. We may not – we don't – have the words with which to compose a theory about what was going on in all that, but we can tell the story of lives that made sense, and try in the telling to make sense of them for ourselves.

From an address given on 5 June 2008 to the Hereford Diocesan Conference.

Michael Ramsey

1904–88

True humanism

It's always entertaining to divide the human race into two categories and decide which group particular people belong to. You're either a little Liberal or else a little Conservative, according to W. S. Gilbert. You're a Roundhead or a Cavalier, a Platonist or an Aristotelean, a Greek or a Hebrew. You belong with Tolstoy or Dostoevsky, Bach or Mozart. You're an optimist or a pessimist (bearing in mind the definition of these terms: the optimist believes that this is the best of all possible worlds, and the pessimist is afraid he's right . . .).

The game can be played with theologians, of course, not least with Anglican theologians. Do you stand with those who see the world as basically God's good creation, with human beings radiating God's image? Or with those who assume that our fallen state is so extreme that the first thing we are aware of is always sin and failure and our need for help from outside? Can we properly use nature and culture to find out about God, or do we depend absolutely on what God tells us through the events of revelation and the pages of the Bible? The former picture is associated with people like Erasmus on the eve of the Reformation, with the great poets and preachers of the seventeenth century, with the Cambridge Platonists and Bishop Westcott and F. D. Maurice and William Temple; the latter with Calvin and the Puritans, with the evangelical revival, or with Kierkegaard's pushing towards the edge of what can be understood by reason and ethics, and with Karl Barth, greatest of all Reformed thinkers in our age.

'Christian humanism' is the name people give to the first picture; the second is sometimes referred to as a 'revelationist' or 'redemptionist' view. But we encounter some obvious problems as soon as we start thinking through both the words used for these views and the actual thinking of the people involved. Calvin had a staggeringly high doctrine of human nature – that's why the failure of human nature was so appalling to him. Bishop Westcott had a profound sense of the evil and corruption in the human heart – that's why the possibility of restoration was so exhilarating. George Herbert was aware of God in the world around, yet he was one of the most searching analysts of human self-deceit and of the need to read the world through the cross of Christ. Karl Barth believed that, in a world where unspeakable tyranny and violence tried to justify itself by appealing to the pattern of creation itself, it was essential to deny that there was any road from the world to God. But the miracle was that God had opened a road from himself to the world and had said yes to it, out of his unforced, free grace, and everything in consequence was alive with his possibilities.

Michael Ramsey wrote a good deal about Christian humanism, one way or another. He produced a very good book on trends in Anglican theology at the end of the nineteenth and the beginning of the twentieth century: *From Gore to Temple. The Development of Anglican Theology between Lux Mundi and the Second World War 1889–1939.*[1] He once delivered an extraordinary tribute to F. D. Maurice. In 1968, he reviewed for *The Spectator* a collection of essays on 'The Humanist Outlook', defending what he considered to be true humanism. And in his Scott Holland Lectures, published under the title of *Sacred and Secular* in 1965, he discussed the 'long and honourable history' of Christian humanism, and the challenges it faced.[2] After a flowering in the Middle Ages, and a huge new opportunity at the Renaissance, this tradition foundered on the rocks of a controversy between religion and science – or rather between 'a religion which distorts its own true character and a scientific theory negligent of science's own manysidedness'.[3]

You might think, then, that if there is anything at all in the polarity between humanism and redemptionism, Ramsey is pretty much on one side of it. Yet, in fact, he offers as much evidence as Barth or Westcott of the relative uselessness of the parlour game we started with. For Ramsey, there is no easy crossover between the wisdom of human culture and the wisdom of God, for the simple reason that God's wisdom is made plain only in the cross. 'In Jesus the human race finds its own true meaning,' he writes in 1969.[4] The cross represents the fact that this meaning is rejected by human beings, but the rejection itself is exactly what makes possible the manifestation of the true glory of humanity and God together.

The cross is the ultimate sign of a love that will not protect itself or hold back; precisely in letting itself be wholly rejected, it can appear as supremely free. When no advantage of power or security is involved, then love can appear as a total giving-away, utterly independent of the world's conditions. A human event becomes the carrier of God's own character, and in that event humanity is shown to be, and enabled to be, the mirror of divine life.

So when Christians engage with the world and with their culture, they don't do so in the hope that they will be readily accepted and that Church and society will flow together in a seamless unity, with no clash of values. Rather, they engage, listen and cooperate, because it is only in the service offered to the world by disinterested love that the action of God becomes manifest.

If the world rejects what the Church offers, so be it; love without conditions means that this has always to be reckoned with as a possibility and even as a gift. To be the servant of the world does not mean being a slavish imitator of the world. Quite the contrary: it is to be so free from the world's definitions that you're free to offer God's love quite independently of your own security or success. Sometimes the world may be in tune and sometimes not; sometimes there is a real symbiosis, sometimes a violent collision. But the labour continues, simply because the rightness of the service does not depend on what the world thinks it wants and whether the world believes it has got what it needs from the Church.

This is to do no more than to paraphrase the Beatitudes. To be 'blessed' is simply to be where God would have you be: if you are aware that there is a place where God would have you be, then your state of mind, your achievement in occupying that place, the effects of your labours, all become irrelevant. 'Rejoice, and be exceeding glad' (Matthew 5.12, KJV): you are where God is, in the place of poverty, humility, peacemaking, suffering and longing for justice, and what matters is to be there faithfully.

'Humanism'? Yes, but a strange variety, we might well say. The final point of human liberty, the ultimate assertion of human dignity, is to be free with God's freedom. What greater affirmation of the dignity of the human creation could there be? But that freedom is the freedom to empty yourself of self-defence and self-deceit; to be there where God is, whatever happens. You can only be a 'humanist' in Ramsey's sense if you are willing to let go of quite a lot of what you think is bound up with your 'human flourishing' – to be converted, in fact, brought into the presence of God's glory in the cross so that in the Holy Spirit the true glory of the human creature may be born in you. 'Man's true glory is the reflection in him of the divine glory, the self-giving love seen in Jesus.'[5]

Michael Ramsey had no interest in dictating to the world what to do or in frustrating the aspirations of reformers. He simply reminded believers of what they had seen and learned in Christ crucified. There is no alibi for service, for being at the disposal of a world full of terrors. There is no promise of a welcome for this service. There is only the twofold Johannine conviction that we must be where he is and that he has promised to be where we are.

An address given on 31 October 2004 at an Evensong service in Magdalene College, Cambridge, to mark the centenary of the birth of Archbishop Michael Ramsey.

Dietrich Bonhoeffer

1906–45

Freedom, necessity and glory

In 1939, the young German theologian Dietrich Bonhoeffer was in New York, exploring whether he should stay there as pastor to the German community in the city and considering a string of invitations to lecture in the United States of America. He had made himself deeply unpopular with the German regime, making broadcasts critical of Hitler and running a secret training institution for pastors in Germany who could not accept the way that the Nazi state was trying to control the Church.

After a draining inner struggle, he decided to sail back to Germany. In July 1939, after little more than a month in New York, he left, knowing that he was returning to a situation of extreme danger. Six years later, he was dead, executed for treason in a concentration camp, leaving behind him one of the greatest treasures of modern Christianity in the shape of the letters he wrote to family and close friends from prison. He had left behind the chance of freedom as most of us would understand it and plunged into a complex and risky world, getting involved in a plot to assassinate Hitler, living as a double agent, daily facing the prospect of arrest, torture and death.

But freedom was one of the things he most often wrote about. In a famous poem he wrote in July 1944, he sketched out what he thought was involved in real freedom: discipline, action, suffering and death. Not quite what we associate with the word – but with these reflections he takes us into the heart of what it is for someone to be lastingly free.

The freedom he is interested in is the freedom to do what we know we have to do. The society we live in will give us all sorts of messages about what we should be doing, and, far more difficult, our own longings and preferences will push us in various directions. We have to watch our own passions and feelings and test them carefully, and then we have to have the courage to act. When we act, we take risks. We seemingly become less free. But what is really happening is that we are handing over our freedom to God and saying, 'I've done what I had to; now it's over to you.' Freedom, he says, is 'perfected in glory' when it's handed over to God.[1] And this finds its climax in the moment of death, when we step forward to discover what has been hidden all along – the eternal freedom of God, underlying everything we have thought and done.

It's a tough and uncompromising picture. But at the end of Bonhoeffer's journey is a vision of the joy that can only come when we discover that we are at last in tune with reality – God's reality. Everything else – the stories we tell ourselves, the pictures of ourselves that we enjoy thinking about, the efforts to make ourselves acceptable – all this falls short of reality. 'The truth will make you free,' says Jesus (John 8.32), and that is what sustained Bonhoeffer in his prison. It's really very like what Jesus talks about in the Beatitudes (Matthew 5.3–10): 'Blessed are the poor, those who are hungry for justice, those who make peace'; these are the people who have got in touch with what eternally matters, with God's reality. These are the free people, because they have been liberated from all the fictions, great and small, that keep us locked into our anxieties and ambitions. These are people not afraid to die, because they have discovered what supremely matters and are willing to hand over everything to God.

There is no forcing of others to accept our vision. It's simply about being detached enough from what makes us comfortable to be able to live out what it takes to show the kind of God that God is, to live in tune with God's freedom, which is always a freedom that makes other people free and gives them joy in the reality, the truth, that is God's life.

It takes time. Bonhoeffer wrote a little guide for students when he ran his college for pastors, in which he explains why they need to give time each day to silent meditation on the Bible. 'God claims our time for this service,' he wrote. 'God needed time before he came to us in Christ. He needs time to come into my heart for my salvation.' Each day we try to open ourselves up to being transformed by this meditation: 'We want to rise from meditation different from what we were when we sat down to it.'[2]

Some religious people talk about letting the surface of our mind settle so that it can truly reflect God, like a still pool. As Bonhoeffer's life and death make clear, this is not some sort of refusal of the world; it is rather the only way we can ever act in the world so as to change it effectively, because we open the way to God's own activity – through us, but not just through us. Looking quietly at all the clutter that prevents us from seeing ourselves honestly, looking quietly at the ways in which the world we live in muffles the truth and so frustrates the search for justice and love – this isn't a luxury. This is how the truth makes us free. Not free to do what we fancy at any given moment, but free to be real, to be truthful, to be 'in the truth', as the New Testament puts it. After all, what other sort of freedom is finally worth having? It may cost us everything we thought we needed to hang on to, but – as the history of Christ's journey to the cross and the resurrection makes clear – the end of the story is a fulfilment, a homecoming, for which we can never find adequate words. It's the freedom to be what we most deeply are.

A sermon preached on 26 February 2012 at The King's School, Canterbury.

Simone Weil
1909–43
Waiting on God

Simone Weil was born in 1909 and died, still a young woman, in 1943 at Ashford in Kent. She had fled from France when the Nazis took over, and spent her last months as a refugee in Britain. Her death was partly the result of her decision that she would eat no more food than was available to the poorest of her fellow citizens in France; it was a decision deeply typical of her single-mindedness.

Simone was Jewish but came from a very secular family; she had never been used to Jewish practice of any kind and the family were encouraged to think of themselves as ordinary French people. But they were not particularly ordinary: Simone's brother, André, was one of the greatest mathematicians of the twentieth century, and Simone herself displayed a precocious gift for philosophy and languages. She had a short period teaching in a high school and another working in a factory because she thought she ought to experience what the most disadvantaged people in her society were experiencing. She had another very brief period attempting to work with the government forces during the Spanish Civil War. But the history of all these brief experiments underlines that she was a spectacularly impractical person who lived most of her life on a level of abstraction and absent-mindedness. She was not exactly the most successful of schoolteachers, let alone factory workers; and she was invalided out of the Spanish forces after two weeks, having managed to put her foot in a pan of boiling chip fat . . .

The intensity of her life is manifest in everything she ever wrote; she was somebody to whom ideas were literally more important than food and drink. As she developed through her teaching and identification with the powerless workers of the Renault factory, she may not have acquired much in the way of practical skill, but this intensely intellectual person had her frontiers broken down. Her intellectualism enlarged and expanded and she encountered a kind of mystery at the heart of things, which her rather comfortable and very clever French bourgeois family hadn't really prepared her for.

She started going on retreats, one of them, when she was in her twenties, at the great Benedictine abbey at Solesmes (a noted centre of liturgy and Gregorian chant). She describes how one evening there she was reciting George Herbert's poem 'Love Bade Me Welcome', which she had learned by heart; as she spoke the words to herself, she wrote, 'Christ himself came down and took possession of me.'[1]

That's almost all she ever says about this experience, but it changed everything. From that point on, all her reflection was oriented around the Christian faith in one way or another. It was a Christian faith that was highly idiosyncratic: she never stopped being immensely intellectually adventurous, and she didn't find it at all easy to go along with conventional Catholic theology. She had a long exchange of letters with one particular Catholic priest and theologian whom she respected, but she always refused to be baptized, because, she said, if she joined the Catholic Church she would feel that she was signing up to the idea that you *had* to join the Catholic Church in order to be saved, and that would leave most of the human race out in the cold. Her conviction was that she needed to stay out in the cold with most of the human race rather than secure her salvation by joining the Church.

Whatever you may make of this, it is at the very least a courageous decision, and one that has its own integrity. It certainly did not stop her reflecting intensely on Christ and the Trinity, the Eucharist, the role of faith in the modern world, and 'the need for roots' (which became the title of one of her books) in a confused and competitive modern society. In the middle of wartime France, she was writing about what France was going to need after the war was over. For her, the most important thing it was going to need was to understand where it had come from and how it needed to reconnect with the natural order and to turn away from the impersonal, technological totalitarianism that controlled the sort of life that she had seen in the factory – a system of power which, to her mind, threatened and overwhelmed real humanity.

Over against that impersonal technological ideal, she defined her own spiritual ideal, casting it regularly in terms of one particular French word which is difficult to translate because it means two things: *attente*, meaning both 'waiting' and 'attention'. It's the kind of waiting experienced by a birdwatcher: you have to be very still, relaxed and focused all at the same time. At every moment you're expecting something, but you're not so screwing up your energies that you are too tensely concentrated to notice when it happens. Her best-known book has the title *Attente de Dieu* (*Waiting on God*): the essence of prayer begins in attention, waiting attention; and this involves a kind of selflessness. You put your thoughts and anxieties on the back burner, you open yourself to what's *there* and you allow your mind to be shaped by what's in front of you.

That is her most central and important idea, and what is most striking about her development of it is that it helps her connect experiences that we all share in some way with the experience of contemplating God. Instead of thinking, 'I must be very concentrated and pure and saintly before I can contemplate God,' we can think, 'I'm actually already "contemplating" in some way when I'm learning how to speak Italian, how to conduct an experiment, even how to ride a bicycle. I am already not unfamiliar with the experience of putting my ego's preoccupations on hold while I respond to the demands of what is simply there, what is simply Not-Me, insisting that I conform my mind and will to its reality.'

As with many of the writers we've considered in this book, there lies behind this a deep theoretical background, and some of the ideas in that background are not easy to digest or come to terms with. Simone sees this selfless process of 'giving ourselves' to our work as the ground of union with God, because God himself is always giving himself so selflessly that we could almost say he cancels himself out so that the world can exist. He steps out of sight so that the world can come into sight. And this gift in which God gives so completely that he virtually cancels out himself as giver is translated by Weil into the idea that somehow our own ideal relationship with God is when we, in response to God's stepping right out of sight, 'cancel' ourselves and are simply aligned with God. As she puts it, we 'de-create' ourselves.

That is the point at which a Christian – or, indeed, a practising Jew – might very well have problems, and it is one of the most contested and argued-over bits of her legacy: why should God create at all if the purpose of creation were only to cancel the life of creation? But the fundamental point about the disciplines of giving yourself over to something other than yourself in order to learn and be made alive in new ways still stands.

The power and density of her writing is almost addictive, so wide and deep is the range of her mind. Her tragedy is that she clearly found it almost impossible to believe that she could or should be loved – partly because of the conviction that her own specific identity always had to be set aside. It also explains a little what seems to be her staggering insensitivity about Judaism, about which she wrote with hostility and incomprehension, as if her own Jewish identity was another embarrassing bit of particularity that needed to be abolished. Yet she never lost sight of that moment when Christ 'came down and took possession' of her as she meditated on those unforgettable words of George Herbert: 'Love bade me welcome, yet my soul drew back, guilty of dust and sin.' At some level, she knew more than she realized, and accepted more than her mind could cope with; and we can only pray that the realization was given to her at the last.

From a lecture given during Holy Week 2009 in Canterbury Cathedral.

Etty Hillesum

1914–43

A compulsion to kneel

Etty Hillesum, who died in Auschwitz in 1943, left behind her a journal covering the two years before her deportation and death. It is an extraordinarily full and absorbing document which chronicles a complex sexual and emotional life, a deepening immersion in Rilke and Dostoevsky and a religious conversion of a very unconventional order. Her Jewishness is both a matter of immense significance – this is Holland in the 1940s – and curiously muted as a religious theme. Like others, it is as if she travelled to her roots by a long detour through the religion and imagination of modern Europe. But among much that is arresting in what she writes, the repeated references to 'learning to kneel' give a clue to something of what she understood by 'God'.

Praying is a physically intimate matter. In 1942, she recorded the sheer difficulty of writing about the urge to kneel which 'sometimes pulses through my body, or rather it is as if my body had been meant and made for the act of kneeling . . . It has become a gesture embedded in my body, needing to be expressed from time to time'. And to say this is more embarrassing 'than if I had to write about my love life'.[1] The gesture is demanded by some inner 'welling-up', a sense of 'plenitude' which transforms the grey landscape of dawn into spaciousness.[2] And it is accompanied by a 'listening in' to the self.[3] Yet this listening is and is not a simple scrutiny of the self: 'it is really God who hearkens inside me. The most essential and the deepest in me hearkening unto the most essential and deepest in the other. God to God.' Loving attention to others is a clearing of 'the path toward You in them'.[4]

It is not easy to disentangle exactly what is being said in all this. Etty Hillesum can speak of thanking God for indwelling her[5] and writes in relation to St Augustine, 'Truly those are the only love letters one ought to write: love letters to God.'[6] God is regularly invoked as source and giver. It would be wrong to read her as simply identifying God with a dimension of the self, something contained in the self, yet it is clear that her sense of God is inseparable from the sense of something growing 'inside'. She quotes approvingly Rilke's *Das Stunden-Buch*: '*Auch wenn wir nicht wollen: Gott reift*' ('Even if we don't want it: God ripens')[7] – the conclusion of a long section dealing with the growth of a sort of divine image in us.

What the journals present is a process of impassioned discovery. Her prayers, in the entries for these days, are exceptionally vivid and immediate; again we find the emphasis on kneeling, 'almost naked, in the middle of the floor, completely "undone"',[8] the struggle to be 'faithful' to God, and, above all, the sense of accumulating something, growing in a way that carries a sort of responsibility. This is a life in which a task is accepted: a task that can be defined only as that of allowing God to 'ripen' in increasingly visible ways.

What this involves comes more plainly to light in the harrowing letters from the transit camp at Westerbork. She had written earlier of accepting suffering as 'passive activity', of the need to accept suffering that is in no sense chosen, including the trials that come from genetic and temperamental givens.[9] She quotes André Suarès on Dostoevsky: 'Pain is not the site of our longing, but the site of our certainty',[10] meaning that suffering is neither to be mastered nor to be fled but to be utilized and transformed. The 'site' is given: unavoidable suffering is what it is, not a stimulus to a longing for a better place or a pedagogy for moral improvement, but a datum which our humanity must humanize.

It is this that perhaps helps us understand what is going on in her thinking about God: the self develops as a place where certain realities can find a home, realities that are in one sense very much the inner business of the self and yet are unsought, not generated by the will or the imagination, but implanted – could we say? – by a life history.

A perceptive commentator has candidly reported her occasional frustration at the lack of what might be thought a proper anger here; I am less sure. The letters from Westerbork leave no ambiguity about her sensations of horror and disgust and, I think, anger at the atrocities she witnesses. But we have to take very seriously the imagery of giving space. She is wholly persuaded that she has a task of internal housekeeping for her imagination and emotion that is to do with guaranteeing that certain things do not disappear from the human landscape. If anger drives out grief, something has disappeared that has the capacity to remake broken human bonds, because grief can be recognized and shared across a conflict, and anger can't. Most decisively, what she believes she is doing is what can best be described as taking responsibility for God in the situation.

> You cannot help us . . . we must help You to help ourselves. And that is all we can manage these days and

also all that really matters: that we safeguard that little piece of You, God, in ourselves.[11]

There must be someone to live through it all and bear witness to the fact that God lived, even in these times. And why should I not be that witness?[12]

From the Romanes Lecture given on 18 November 2004 in Oxford. Published in ch. 26 of Faith in the Public Square, *copyright © 2012 Bloomsbury Continuum, an imprint of Bloomsbury Publishing plc. Reproduced by permission.*

St Óscar Romero

1917–80

God has injected himself into history

Sentir con la Iglesia ('Feeling with the Church'). This was Óscar Romero's motto as a bishop – we see it in many photographs inscribed on the episcopal mitre he wore. It is in fact an ancient phrase, very often used to express the ideal state of mind for a loyal Catholic Christian; indeed, it's usually been translated as '*thinking* with the Church'. It can be used and has been used simply to mean having the same sentiments as the Church's teaching authority.

But the life and death of Monseñor Romero take us to a far deeper level of meaning. Here was a man who was by no means a temperamental revolutionary. For all his compassion and pastoral dedication, for all the intensity of his personal spirituality as a young priest and later as a bishop, he seems originally to have been one of those who would have interpreted *sentir con la Iglesia* essentially in terms of loyalty to the teaching and good order of the Church. And for all the affection he inspired, many remembered him in his earlier ministry as a priest who was a true friend to the poor – but also a friend of the rich. In the mordant phrase of one observer, 'His thinking was that the sheep and the wolves should eat from the same dish.'

His breakthrough into a more complete and more demanding vision came, of course, as a result of seeing at close quarters what the wolves were capable of, and so realizing the responsibility of the shepherd in such a situation. The conversion that began with the vicious slaughter of innocent peasants by the Salvadoran National Guard in 1974 and 1975 came to its decisive climax with the murder of his Jesuit friend Rutilio Grande in March 1977, a few weeks after Romero's installation as Archbishop. From that moment on, *sentir con la Iglesia* had a new meaning and a deeply biblical one. 'The poor broke his heart,' said Jesuit priest Jon Sobrino, 'and the wound never closed.'

'Feeling with the Church' meant, more and more clearly, sharing the agony of Christ's body, the body that was being oppressed, raped, abused and crucified over and over again by one of the most ruthless governments in the Western hemisphere. In the early summer of the same year, 1977, in the wake of the atrocities committed by government forces at Aguilares, he spoke to the people in plain terms: 'You are the image of the divine victim . . . You are Christ today, suffering in history.'

These words were uttered in a town where the soldiers had shot open the tabernacle in the church and left the floor littered with consecrated hosts. There could be no more powerful a sign of what was going on in terms of the war of the state against the body of Christ.

Romero knew that in this war the only weapons of the body were non-violent ones, and he never spared his criticisms of those revolutionaries who resorted to terror and whose murderous internal factionalism and fighting were yet another wound in the suffering body of the people. For him, the task of the Church was not to be a subsidiary agency of any faction but to be the voice of that suffering body.

And so his question to all those who have the freedom to speak in the Church and for the Church is, 'Who do you really speak for?' But if we take seriously the underlying theme of his words and witness, that question is also, 'Who do you really feel with?' Are you immersed in the real life of the body, or is your life in Christ seen only as having the same sentiments as the powerful? *Sentir con la Iglesia*, in the sense in which the mature Romero learned those words, is what will teach you how to speak on behalf of the body. And we must make no mistake about what this can entail: Romero knew that this kind of 'feeling with the Church' could only mean taking risks with and for the body of Christ – so that, as he later put it, in words that are still shocking and sobering, it would be 'sad' if priests in such a context were not being killed alongside their flock. As, of course, they were in El Salvador, again and again in those nightmare years.

But Romero never suggested that speaking on behalf of the body is the responsibility of a spiritual elite. He never dramatized the role of the priest so as to play down the responsibility of the people. If every priest and bishop were silenced, he said, 'Each one of you will have to be a microphone of God; each one of you will have to be a messenger and a prophet. The church will always exist as long as there is even one baptized person, and that one baptized person remaining in the world will be responsible for holding up to the world the Lord's banner of truth and of divine justice.'[1] Each part of the body, because it shares the sufferings of the whole – and the hope and radiance of the whole – has authority to speak out of that common life in the crucified and risen Jesus.

So Romero's question and challenge is addressed to all of us, not only to those who have the privilege of some sort of public megaphone for their voices. The Church is maintained in truth, and the whole Church has to be a community where truth is told about the abuses of power and the cries of the vulnerable.

On one occasion when Romero was returning from abroad, an official at the airport said loudly as he passed, 'There goes the truth.' It is hard to think of a better tribute to any Christian. If we believe that the Church is graced with the Spirit of Truth, we need to remember that this is not about a supernatural assurance that will tell us abstract truths: it is, according to our Lord in the Gospel of John, a truth that 'convicts' (John 16.8), a truth that exposes us to a divine presence, a light that will show us who we are and what the world is and where our values are adrift. The Church has to be truly the dwelling place of the Spirit by becoming a place where suffering and injustice are named for what they are. It may not make for a superficially placid Church, but only when truth about human pain is allowed an honest voice can there be healing for the Church or the world. The deepest unity of the body is created by Christ's own embrace without reservation of the appalling suffering, the helplessness and voicelessness, the guilt, the frustration, the self-doubt of human beings, so as to infuse into it his own divine compassion. With Christ, said Romero in a Christmas sermon, 'God has injected himself into history'.

If that is the foundation for the unity of the body, a true martyr-saint is someone who does not belong to a faction or party in the Church, who is not just a simple hero for left or right, but one who expresses clearly and decisively the embrace of Christ offered to all who suffer, who struggle, who fear to be lost and fear even more to be found. It is an embrace offered to all, including those who are trapped in their own violence and inhumanity: it is good news for the rich as well as the poor. But the embrace of Christ for the prosperous, let alone the violent, is not a matter of getting sheep and wolves to mingle freely; it is an embrace that fiercely lays hold of sinners and will not let go until love has persuaded them to let go of their power and privilege.

That was the love out of which Monseñor Romero spoke in his last sermon when he urged the soldiers of the government to lay down their arms rather than obey unjust orders, and commanded the rulers of El Salvador to stop the murder and repression. That was the love that provoked exactly what the love of our Lord provoked – that ultimate testimony to the emptiness and impotence of violent power that is murder. Organized evil has no final sanction except death, and when death is seen, accepted and undergone for the sake of the only true power in the universe, which is God's love, organized evil is helpless. It is exposed as having nothing to say or do, exposed as unreal, for all its horrific ingenuity and force. 'Life has the last word,' said the great Gustavo Gutiérrez, preaching in 1995 in memory of the martyrs of El Salvador.

And as we give thanks for Óscar Romero's witness to life, the life of Christ in his body, we are left with the questions that Jesus puts to us again and again, in his own words, his death and resurrection, but also in the life and death of his saints and martyrs: 'Whose is the voice you speak with? Whose are the needs you speak for? What is the truth you embody?'

From a sermon preached on 28 March 2010 at a service in Westminster Abbey to mark the 30th anniversary of the martyrdom of Archbishop Óscar Romero.

Notes

St Paul

1 See M. R. James, *The Apocryphal New Testament* (Oxford: Oxford University Press (revised) 1960), pp. 272–81 for the story of Paul and Thekla – a sort of historical novel about Paul. The description is on page 273.

St Alban

1 See Bede, *Ecclesiastical History of the English People* (Kindle edition, Penguin, 2003), Book I, chapter 7.

St Augustine of Canterbury

1 See Bede, *Ecclesiastical History of the English People* (Kindle edition, Penguin, 2003), Book II, chapter 1.

St Anselm of Canterbury

1 Passages from the 'Meditation on Human Redemption'; see Benedicta Ward (trans.), *The Prayers and Meditations of Saint Anselm* (Harmondsworth: Penguin Books, 1973), pp. 230–7.

Meister Eckhart

1 Maurice O'C. Walshe (trans.), *The Complete Mystical Works of Meister Eckhart* (New York: Herder and Herder, 2009), pp. 293–4.

Thomas Cranmer

1 Brian Cummings (ed.), *The Book of Common Prayer: The Texts of 1549, 1559, and 1662* (Oxford: Oxford University Press, 2011), pp. 251, 262, 455.
2 Cummings (ed.), *The Book of Common Prayer*, p. 402.

3 Thomas Cranmer, *Writings of the Rev. Dr. Thomas Cranmer, Archbishop of Canterbury* (London: The Religious Tract Society, 1831), p. 67.

4 Cranmer, *Writings of the Rev. Dr. Thomas Cranmer*, p. 67.

William Tyndale

1 William Tyndale, *Doctrinal Treatises and Introductions to Different Portions of the Holy Scriptures* (Cambridge: Cambridge University Press, 1848), p. 20.

2 Tyndale, *Doctrinal Treatises*, p. 98.

3 Tyndale, *Doctrinal Treatises*, p. 99.

4 Tyndale, *Doctrinal Treatises*, p. 99.

St Teresa of Avila

1 Teresa of Avila, *The Way of Perfection*, chapter 27.

2 Author's own translation from the Spanish.

3 Mirabai Starr (trans.), *Teresa of Avila: The Book of My Life* (Boston: New Seeds Books, 2007), pp. 73–4.

4 E. Allison Peers (trans., ed.), *St. Teresa of Avila: Interior Castle* (New York: Dover Publications Inc, 1946), p. 148.

5 Peers (trans., ed.), *St. Teresa of Avila: Interior Castle*, pp. 165–6.

John Milton

1 John Milton, Elijah Fenton, Sam Barrow, Samuel Johnson, Andrew Marvell, *Paradise Lost* (London: John Bumpus, Holborn-Bars, 1821), p. 378.

2 Milton et al, *Paradise Lost*, p. 3.

3 Milton et al, *Paradise Lost*, p. 384.

4 Milton et al, *Paradise Lost*, p. 383.

5 John Milton, *Paradise Regain'd: A Poem in Four Books* (London: T. Cadell, Jun. and W. Davies, 1795), pp. 255–6.

6 Milton, *Paradise Regain'd*, p. 256.

7 Milton, *Paradise Regain'd*, p. 259

8 Milton, *Paradise Regain'd*, p. 57.

Charles Dickens

1 Charles Dickens, *Bleak House*, chapter 47.
2 Dickens, *Bleak House*, chapter 58.
3 Charles Dickens, *The Life of Our Lord: Written for His Children During the Years 1846 to 1849*, chapter 11.

Michael Ramsey

1 London: Longman, 1965.
2 Michael Ramsey, *Sacred and Secular* (London: Longman, 1965).
3 Ramsey, *Sacred and Secular*, p. 69.
4 Michael Ramsey, *God, Christ and the World* (London: SCM Press, 1969), p. 100.
5 Ramsey, *God, Christ and the World*, p. 100.

Dietrich Bonhoeffer

1 Dietrich Bonhoeffer, 'Stations on the Road to Freedom' (1944).
2 Dietrich Bonhoeffer, *The Way to Freedom* (London: Collins, 1966), p. 58.

Simone Weil

1 Simone Weil, *Waiting on God* (London: Fontana Books, 1959), p. 35.

Etty Hillesum

1 Klaas A. D. Smelik (ed.), Arnold J. Pomerans (trans.), *Etty: The Letters and Diaries of Etty Hillesum, 1941–1943* (Grand Rapids: Wm. B. Eerdmans Publishing Company, 2002), p. 320.
2 Smelik and Pomerans, *Etty*, p. 216.
3 Smelik and Pomerans, *Etty*, p. 212.
4 Smelik and Pomerans, *Etty*, p. 519.
5 For example, Smelik and Pomerans, *Etty*, p. 237.
6 Smelik and Pomerans, *Etty*, p. 546.
7 Smelik and Pomerans, *Etty*, p. 192.
8 Smelik and Pomerans, *Etty*, p. 497.

9 Smelik and Pomerans, *Etty*, pp. 160–1.
10 Smelik and Pomerans, *Etty*, p. 183.
11 Smelik and Pomerans, *Etty*, p. 488.
12 Smelik and Pomerans, *Etty*, p. 506.

St Óscar Romero

1 Joseph V. Owens SJ (trans.), *A Prophetic Bishop Speaks to his People: The Complete Homilies of Archbishop Oscar Arnulfo Romero, vol. 5* (Miami: Convivium Press, 2016), p. 97.

Tyler's Story

A little story about learning to read in prison

It's probably my drinking that got me into prison. That and not having a proper job.

I wasn't bothered about school, but in prison I had a chance to join a reading group. The books are interesting but not too hard to read.

In one book, *Forty-six Quid and a Bag of Dirty Washing*, we read about Barry, a guy who got mixed up with a drug dealer, but has now just left prison. I saw how he had to make good choices every day – and fill in lots of forms – to stay out of prison. I don't want to end up back inside again, so I've decided that I'm not going to drink on my way home. I won't get home drunk before the evening's even started – that just makes me drink more. And I'm going to get better at reading so I can fill in forms when I get out.

Inspired by a true story. Names have been changed.

Help us to tell more stories like Tyler's. Support the Diffusion Fiction Project. Just £4.99 puts an easy-to-read book in prisoners' hands, to help them to improve their reading confidence while encouraging them to think about life's big questions. Visit www.spck.org.uk to make a donation or, to volunteer to run a reading group in a prison, please contact prisonfiction@spck.org.uk.